PRAISE FOR *LEAN STARTUP, TO LEAN COMPANY, TO RICH EXIT*

I really enjoyed reading Kenan Sahin's book. His life, as well as this book, are what successful scientific entrepreneurship is all about. Starting with hardly any funds, he built a company that was acquired by Lucent for over a billion dollars. Dr. Sahin provides many lessons and stories that I expect will be of great value to any entrepreneur regardless of what business they want to create.

—Professor Robert Langer
Institute Professor, Massachusetts Institute of Technology

This book is an unusual, and unusually compelling, contribution to the literature on innovation, leadership, and strategy. It is, most immediately, a heartfelt human story of courage, invention, growth, learning and reflection, and extraordinary impact. This human dimension extends further to the way that a company, if well run, can affect deeply the lives of its employees and other stakeholders. And we are reminded that organizations are the way that ideas change the world.

As to the ideas, the book offers excellent advice and insights for creating and sustaining a culture of innovation, for leading with values and authenticity, and for continued success in one of the most competitive and dynamic sectors. This is a useful, engaging, and fulfilling read.

—David Schmittlein
John C Head III Dean, MIT Sloan School of Management

Kenan Sahin is a legend. I remember hearing about the Kenan Systems' exit and being shocked. It was and still is today the gold standard. In this well-written book, he humbly pulls back the curtain in an honest way, including exposing vulnerabilities, to reveal how it happens. It was not an accident and there are valuable lessons to be learned. A must read for all aspiring entrepreneurs.

—Bill Aulet
Ethernet Inventors Professor of the Practice of Entrepreneurship, MIT Sloan School of Management

Managing Director, Martin Trust Center for MIT Entrepreneurship

Author, Disciplined Entrepreneurship: 24 Steps to a Successful Startup

Kenan has always been a technology and innovation optimist, and this thoughtful book is a testament to that commitment. Throughout his journey he has garnered valuable experiences in entrepreneurship, business futures, and what it takes to succeed. Read this book and, most importantly, learn from it so humanity profits from your work!

—Larry Weber

Founder and CEO, Racepoint Global

Founder, Weber Shandwick

Very few entrepreneurs go from bootstrap to success on the scale that Kenan Sahin has. Even fewer are also teachers who can mine the trials and tribulations of creating, cultivating, and growing a business and extract insights applicable to virtually any venture. That's what Sahin has done with this wonderful book. It's packed with anecdotes and lessons from an incredible journey that began with $1,000 and eventually led to the greatest philanthropic gift in MIT's history. It's a story "from start up to gratitude" that is not to be missed.

—Robert Buderi

Former Editor in Chief, MIT Technology Review

Author, Where Futures Converge: Kendall Square and the Making of a Global Innovation Hub

Kenan Sahin built a remarkable company following the mantra of a good teacher: By your students you'll be taught. Paying attention to what he was learning as a consultant and a teacher at MIT, he turned much management theory on its head and continued to learn with his management team. *Lean Startup, To Lean Company, To Rich Exit* draws on his learning from the experience of Kenan Systems, the company he founded and managed along that path. Using striking parables to illuminate innovative management solutions, he shows how talent can be recruited, organized, and engaged in building a successful business in a rapidly changing technology and market environment while working hard and having what they describe as the best times of their lives. A terrific read.

—Joseph L. Bower
Donald Kirk David Professor of Business Administration Emeritus, Harvard Business School

Kenan is a multifaceted person: an intellectual, a professor, an entrepreneur, wealth creator, philanthropist, and a turnaround professional. He is a complete person, and his life story has many very useful stories for anyone who wants to impact the world with their entrepreneurial zeal.

Dr. Gururaj "Desh" Deshpande
Cofounder, Sycamore Networks

President and Chairman, Spart Group, LLC

Cofounder, Deshpande Center for Technological Innovation at MIT

LEAN STARTUP,
TO LEAN COMPANY,
TO RICH EXIT

LEAN STARTUP, TO LEAN COMPANY, TO RICH EXIT

HOW TO APPLY KENAN SYSTEMS'

$1,000 IN, $1.5 BILLION OUT PRINCIPLES

TO TODAY'S STARTUPS

KENAN E. SAHIN, PhD

Forbes | Books

Published by Forbes Books, Charleston, South Carolina.
An imprint of Advantage Media Group.

Forbes Books is a registered trademark, and the Forbes Books colophon is a trademark of Forbes Media, LLC.

Printed in the United States of America.

10 9 8 7 6 5 4 3 2 1

ISBN: 979-8-88750-249-6 (Hardcover)
ISBN: 979-8-88750-250-2 (eBook)

Library of Congress Control Number: 2023922729

Cover design by Matthew Morse.
Layout design by Ruthie Wood.

This custom publication is intended to provide accurate information and the opinions of the author in regard to the subject matter covered. It is sold with the understanding that the publisher, Forbes Books, is not engaged in rendering legal, financial, or professional services of any kind. If legal advice or other expert assistance is required, the reader is advised to seek the services of a competent professional.

Since 1917, Forbes has remained steadfast in its mission to serve as the defining voice of entrepreneurial capitalism. Forbes Books, launched in 2016 through a partnership with Advantage Media, furthers that aim by helping business and thought leaders bring their stories, passion, and knowledge to the forefront in custom books. Opinions expressed by Forbes Books authors are their own. To be considered for publication, please visit **books.Forbes.com**.

CONTENTS

PROLOGUE

January 26, 1999. News outlets in Boston and around the world announced in bold headlines that *Kenan Systems Corporation* had been sold to Lucent Technologies for $1.54 billion in stock, all paid up front without any caveats or golden handcuffs on the company founder who was free to walk the next day. The stock was convertible to cash after only thirty days.

Only thirteen deals were larger in a yeasty year for acquisitions that saw 10,892 of them in the United States, and this was the only deal of this magnitude where the founder was also the sole shareholder—a feat not achieved before and possibly not since.[1]

I am Kenan Sahin, that founder and CEO. This book is about Kenan Systems being launched as a Lean Startup with $1,000, evolving into a Lean Company, and seventeen years later achieving a Rich Exit.

Also unprecedented was Lucent, which owned and operated Bell Labs, agreeing to hire the seven hundred technical staff of Kenan Systems as Members of Bell Labs Staff (MBLS), a highly coveted position in the century-old crown jewel of American research and development.

Kenan Systems had built several early artificial intelligence (AI) systems and parlayed those into its marquee product, the ARBOR Telecommunications Billing and Customer Care Platform, which today services more than a billion telecom customers, or about a third of the global subscribers.

Rich Exit and Big Impact

For a startup business to succeed as Kenan Systems did, a long string of independent events needs to turn out just right. Luck is no doubt a big factor. However, if each of these events is handled well and iteratively a framework is developed, then the outcome is more in the hands of the founders.

This book will articulate such a framework that layer by layer and step by step guided Kenan Systems. I am a former academic, and in that role one tries to go from the specific to the general. Thus my ambitious objective for this book is to evolve the specifics of the Kenan Systems journey to a framework of principles, which can be viewed as a formula, that can guide an aspiring entrepreneur's journey from Lean Startup to Lean Company to Rich Exit with Big Impact.

Kenan E. Sahin, PhD
Lexington, Massachusetts

INTRODUCTION

When Lucent came knocking on the door of our Cambridge office, we had grown our little Kenan Systems startup into a sizable company with offices in Denver, Washington, DC, Coral Gables, Princeton, Sao Paolo, Buenos Aires, London, Paris, Madrid, Munich, and Singapore. Our clients included AT&T, US West, Citibank, United States Postal Service (USPS), British Telecom, France Telecom, Vodafone, Telefonica, and so on.

Our expansion had been accelerated by both the Telecommunications Act of 1996 and the explosive growth of internet commerce. We were working with system integration partners like IBM, Price Waterhouse, EDS, and Ernst & Young, and were in deep discussions with Bellcore. With all of this going on, I was quite intentionally trying to fly under the Wall Street radar, which I will explain a little later.

However, in the summer of 1998, I received a call from Lucent Technologies, which had been spun off from AT&T and had become the new home of Bell Labs, an organization I knew and adored. I took the call. Right away I made it clear I was not interested in investments but in seeking system integrator partners. The caller assured me that Lucent was seeking partnership.

We agreed to meet.

On the appointed day the representatives of Lucent showed up in multiple limos and sharp suits. I realized they had a different notion of partnering. At least ten people poured out of those limos

1

including Lucent group president of Communications Software, Carl Hsu. When we'd all found seats in our conference room, Carl said that Lucent wanted to acquire us.

I rather strongly pushed back.

Carl then wanted to meet with me one on one. He asked if I knew how big such a transaction could be. I responded that I did. (The market multiples of earnings—EBITDA or earnings before interest, taxes, depreciation, amortization—for acquisitions at that time were reaching into the thirties, with Lucent's approaching fifty. While I did not tell him my estimate, since I knew our company earnings and the prevailing multiples, the value would be well over a billion dollars.) They left surprised and clearly disappointed.

A few months later, I was in Europe meeting with executives at British Telecom, Telefonica, and France Telecom—our flagship customers—alongside AT&T, MCI WorldCom, and Quest—but I felt a little overwhelmed.

The little company, started on a shoestring $1,000 in 1982 and only 750 employees strong by 1999, would still be hard-pressed to service all of the large global companies that we were lining up.

I had hired an exceptional staff that shone to the heavens, quite frankly, in their creation of new AI-based Big Data systems. Would our current business configuration essentially force these talents to spend most of their time maintaining the systems we were installing all over the world, instead of working on new applications that could break new ground?

We clearly needed a whole lot more corporate muscle than we had ... even though every fiber of my being resisted getting swallowed up by a big rich outfit like Lucent.

Then suddenly it hit me: I might not have to fold Kenan Systems into Lucent. I might be able to *merge* it into the legendary Bell Labs, technically. That would be something, surely! Plus, we had much more in common with Bell Labs, which was leading the telecom revolution with its dazzling inventions. Kenan Systems would have a safe harbor in Lucent and our exceptional staff could thrive within the innovation hotbed of Bell Labs.

What a grand idea! Except that it was hard enough for a single person to get hired by Bell Labs, but the entire technical staff of Kenan Systems?!

Nothing ventured, nothing gained, I figured. So, I ran the idea first to Howard Johnson who chaired our Board (among his many distinctions, Howard was the former president of MIT and later chairman of its Board). Howard agreed it was an audacious proposition, but why not? I then called Lucent's group president Carl Hsu from a pay phone in London. He too thought it was a tall order but agreed to run it up his ladder to Rich McGinn, CEO of Lucent, and Dan Stanzione, president of Bell Labs.

Within the month they blew me away. The answer was … yes.

It was a "careful what you wish for" moment, but there was now no backing away. The course was set. So first off, what was Kenan Systems worth?

Projected EBITDA for 1999 was around $110 million with an estimated growth rate of around 50 percent in 2000.

With the EBITDA multiples of thirty to forty for the likes of Kenan Systems, the fair market value was at least $3 billion, confirming what the investment bankers at JP Morgan had penciled out. Price was a secondary concern to me. While I pursued generating good revenue, my primary focus was validating my own core business models that could make a big impact on business, and even become transformational. What could be a better ecosystem to achieve that than Lucent and Bell Labs? It was like being allowed behind the curtain of America's greatest innovation machine.

Beyond my wildest expectations and dreams.

But how could our 750-person company, no matter how excellent, operate successfully in this 136,000-employee company with its long and storied history of inventive genius and still be impactful?

It was a simply audacious proposition

Nonetheless, I went for it and asked for "special" nonmonetary conditions. For the first year, I would continue to run Kenan Systems as a wholly owned subsidiary of Lucent and our technical staff would all become MBLS. Later I more fully realized how audacious this ask was. At the time, Bell Labs had about a five thousand head count. It was laborious to hire just one person into this august community that shunned titles—just being known as MBLS was enough. I was asking they wholesale hire seven hundred of my technical colleagues—each one getting that coveted MBLS distinction.

All I wanted were these special conditions along with around $1.5 billion for the deal, nearly a 50 percent discount from the market value as assessed by JP Morgan. Sure, it was still one of the biggest deals of the year, but more importantly it was an opportunity to preserve the company we'd built over seventeen years and possibly make a great impact on the American business landscape together with Lucent and Bell Labs.

Because in acquiring Kenan Systems, Lucent was also acquiring our business models and practices. And that was no small thing. We had developed layers of principles about business innovation that could energetically complement Bell Labs' technical innovations.

Drawing on my previous years teaching at MIT, I was aspiring to marry innovation engineering with organizational engineering. No longer just teaching or pontificating about it in the classroom, but actually implementing it from within the amazing ecosystem of Lucent/Bell Labs.

Kenan Systems already had a solid track record in this regard. We had played a role in turning around the IT productivity paradox that had haunted the 1980s and early 1990s. That is, billions had been spent on IT systems yet no real productivity gains had come from it. Analysts estimated gains through 1995 from IT spending at 0.5–1.1 percent on the low end, 1.6–2.7 percent on the high end.[2] Not impressive. But our Kenan Systems' innovations in organizational structure and operations had delivered productivity gains measured in double digits year after year.

Indeed, this was validated when we found Kenan Systems product lines in our first year with Lucent contributing 5 percent of the company's total net cash despite comprising only 0.7 percent of their employees. In fun terms, we were punching about seven times above our weight.

In time our flagship ARBOR software that we'd developed for the telecommunications sector would serve more than a billion telecom customers, or a third of the entire global market.

Many years would pass before I came to fully appreciate how rare this business transaction had been in the annals of US industry. My thoughts were focused on whether others could use the technical and organizational innovations and learnings of Kenan Systems and replicate the transformation of Lean Startup to Lean Company to Rich Exit—hence this book.

Following our merger into Lucent, I realized I needed to recognize that I'd benefited enormously from my affiliation with MIT as a student and professor.

At MIT's big fundraising gala in the fall of 1999 an unorthodox idea sprang into my head, like the light bulb moment the year before in London—merging Kenan Systems into Bell Labs. I found myself asking MIT president Dr. Chuck Vest to give me a minute at the mic so I could announce my idea.

He agreed reluctantly, knowing better than to trust one of his former academics with unscripted time in front of the potential donors. My heart began to race. I had just formulated this idea and didn't yet have the words for it. Was I really going to act so ... impulsively?

Grabbing hold of the podium as tightly as I could, I asked that four people—Dr. Chuck Vest, MIT president; Howard Johnson, former MIT president; Dr. Paul Gray, former MIT president; and Alex d'Arbeloff, chairman of the Board for MIT—be put in charge of deciding how MIT would spend the $100 million unrestricted gift I was at that moment making to MIT.

A sudden stillness spread over the room—shocked uncertainty.

How could this be real? It would be the largest gift ever to MIT, possibly the largest ever to any university at that time. Indeed, the *Wall Street Journal* called the evening "only the beginning of a wave of stock-market-fueled philanthropy bigger than any since the days of the Carnegies, Vanderbilts and Rockefellers."[3]

I called it gratitude.

1

LAUNCHING A LEAN STARTUP

Everything begins with motivation

In the subsequent chapters, I will chronicle the ups and downs, the insights, the learnings, and the teachings of the journey from startup to gratitude, weaving it all into a general, context-based framework for others to apply.

I believe this will help the aspiring entrepreneur enter the journey with more confidence, or possibly more caution or even more apprehension. Forewarned is thus prepared.

Why even start a business and become an entrepreneur? Many motivations come to mind ...

- Taking an amazing invention or product to market

- Making a lot of money

- Not getting rich, but gaining financial independence

- Fame

- Proving Mom and Dad wrong, or making them proud

- Pursuing a passion

- Becoming your own boss

- Giving back

- Building a lasting legacy

- Positively impacting one of society's big challenges

- Having the freedom to work from anywhere

- Interacting with others with similar interests

- Putting food on the table

- Leaving a job you hate for one that couldn't be worse

- No real reason other than it's in your blood, and you must

Each motivation can lead to a different outcome, with some startups getting rich from the get-go with hefty venture capital (VC) backing … others becoming nonprofits that seek to do good work … others trying the "friends and family" funding routes … and still others becoming an adjunct to an existing company.

My motivation?

I had been a professor for nearly a decade and a half teaching undergraduates and graduate students at MIT, Harvard, and the University of Massachusetts in Amherst, as well as mid-level executives coming for a master's degree at MIT. My teaching stints had always been rated excellent. However, increasingly I had self-doubts. I really didn't know if all the things I'd been telling my students were any good at all, because I'd never worked in the so-called real world. Not for a minute. How valid was the content of my teaching? Was it just my way of telling stories?

So I wanted to validate my classroom theories and pontifications about Expert Systems, Big Data-Based Information Systems, and, more broadly, using technology for organizational engineering.

A voice boomed, "Kenan, that is just crap"

My most memorable "students" were the Sloan Fellows, a special class of mid-career executives and professionals coming to MIT to get their master's degree in an intensive, demanding, whirlwind study. (Alfred P. Sloan, an MIT graduate, was the key architect of General Motors in its early days. Sloan Fellows were named after him. In 1964, MIT's School of Industrial Management was renamed MIT Sloan School and is today one of the world's finest business schools, although its DNA is still engineering.)

I was in the middle of my doctoral thesis work the first time I taught the Fellows. With many sleepless nights and skipped meals, I was not the picture of health. And when I popped into the classroom, the Fellows saw a rail-thin kid who looked barely twenty, no doubt the teaching assistant (TA) there to erase the chalkboard, certainly not one of the famed MIT professors. They roundly ignored me and did not stop their loud talking—nothing at all like the usual crop of students.

"Excuse me," I said, "the instructor is here."

You could hear a pin drop. I wasn't at all sure if I put these distinguished-captains-of-industry-turned-temporary-students at ease by launching right away into my pontifications about business, but launch I did.

A few years later, now with more maturity, I was deep into one of my launches that corporate Boards should be strengthened and unchecked CEOs being dangerous to the company and to society.

From the back of the class, a voice boomed, "Kenan, that is just crap."

Everyone froze. In those days, students did not challenge teachers.

I turned to the Fellow and said, "You could be right, but let's ask the class."

Some amazing perspectives quickly emerged. No surprise, since these "students" had been practitioners for years. We blended their insights with my provocations and ended up with erudition.

And from that tense session and many to follow, I learned the power of socializing ideas and blending different viewpoints. Then on, I would begin the first class of the semester by proclaiming that I too am a student and invited them to teach me as well. Teach (them) and learn (from them)—or *Teach & Learn*.

They did a wonderful job.

I did OK as well, for I was later recognized with the Salgo-Noren Award "for teaching excellence as a stimulus and recognition for dedicated and inspirational classroom teachers in the United States," as it says on the award's website.[4]

As the years at MIT Sloan went by, each new class of Fellows began to have more in common with me.

Age.

I was no longer the thin guy mistaken for a TA. I had lost my youthful brio and began experiencing something new—self-doubt. Call it a midlife crisis. Sure, I was only in my thirties, but it felt middle-aged to me.

I had published, as professors do, and with that had come some validation of my pontifications. I had even secured some snazzy patents. But genuine field validation and field implementation I did not have.

Were the theories, inventions, and patents I'd developed and learned around Big Data, information systems, algorithms for decision-making, computer networks, and the like of interest only to academics? Or was there some real business world relevance raring to bust out?

If any of my ideas could even be implemented, could I ever expect to find joy in witnessing their impact?

I had to take my experiments into the field. Had to get validation, to find out if the dog was going to eat the dog food, as they say.

But how was I going to do that? The answer to the question I kept asking myself kept going unanswered.

I had taken some time away from MIT to become a tenured professor at UMass Amherst, but would return part-time to teach the Sloan Fellows. Teaching them and learning from them triggered a big realization—namely that there are real differences between the academic ecosystem and the outside industrial world, yet it is critical for the two to mesh if society is to benefit.

I had spent years enthusiastically pontificating to these Sloan Fellows—captains of industry that included Bill Ford of Ford Motor Company and Kofi Annan, the Secretary General of the United Nations.

But how presumptive had I been?

The doubts were getting louder. Was I just throwing my pontifications I had conjured up, simply made up, or pulled from books against the wall to see what stuck, or was I capably meshing academia and industry?

Why not start a company and find out? Do real field validation. And so I had my own primary motivation for going into business: to move my experiment from the lab to the real world.

A simple experiment it would not be, however. It would become a nearly twenty-year journey from Lean Startup to Lean Company to Rich Exit.

The launch to seek field validation

A company has to have a name. Obvious. Even if the name is *Noname*. In August 1982 in the short break between my classes, I walked across the Longfellow Bridge that connects Cambridge to Boston proper to register a name with the State.

Decision Support Systems was my choice. Alas, the clerk informed me that my choice was too close to names already taken.

After many futile iterations, as a placeholder I proposed *Consultants for Management Decisions*—the best I could do before rushing back for an afternoon class.

My plan to validate my classroom teachings, declarations, and innovative theories in the field was launched. The name quickly evolved into an acronym, *CMD*. Just as well, as the full name was a mouthful and temporary, so I assumed.

Later I was to find out that a name once given takes root. And in due time it becomes shorthand for the persona of the company and in fact might even define it. Giving the matter more time and reflection would have been better, for this haste eventually committed my own name to the newly hatched company.

Then, as now, there were many books, videos, and classes on starting a company. These days, even AI can kick out a business plan for you. But these tools are seldom as helpful as the promoters would have us believe.

That's because startups by their very nature are sailing out onto wide-open oceans. And the business plan that may have worked for

ABC Company will only help with the basics: The water is wet, the water is deep, there are buoys near shore, there are islands charted and not, there are dragons over the horizon.

But from day one on the entrepreneurial journey there will be a thousand unknowns that no business plan, especially one cribbed from the internet, can possibly prepare you for. As Dwight Eisenhower said about preparing for battle, plans are useless, but planning is indispensable. Or said even better by prizefighter Mike Tyson, everyone has a plan until they get punched in the mouth.

And there I've gone with war and sports analogies to talk about facets of entrepreneurship. They work here, but in the larger context of actually being an entrepreneur, I've never viewed it as competing with another guy out there, killing him to capture the market, and make loads of money. A much better analogy for entrepreneurship is gardening. In patiently tending, nurturing up from seedlings, you create a harvest bounty of fruits year after year. You truly create value and "feed" people, make them better off. For which they'll pay!

Getting going in business

A startup really gets going when you do the work of organizing a *portfolio of offers*, as I call them. I speak about what we now call a B2B company—business to business. If you are instead looking to launch a consumer products company, your route will be similar and different at the same time.

Either way, having a portfolio of offers is the thing. By offers I mean your talents, your products, your invention, your business capabilities. The thing you are offering the market. If you have but a single offer, you will be too narrowly targeted and miss many *docking sites* or places it is valued in the market.

Identify an Initial Portfolio of "Offers"

You can expect this portfolio of offers to change over time. That is a good thing, a sign of a maturing business. What matters is that the true north sighting of your initial motivations remains in place. That will keep you on track when oceans of waves cresting ahead of you steal the horizon from your view.

And steal they will!

With my own portfolio in hand, I started exploring the docking sites for my offers through what I call *noisy exploration*; I began banging about rather haphazardly. Not confining myself to well-targeted or scripted market research. And why?

Because the world is full of opportunities that at first appear invisible and only show themselves once we interact with them, once we begin exploring them, once we tell others about them, once we get feedback on them.

This exploration needs to be richly noisy, though not to the point of unwieldy. Just enough so that many opportunities become visible ...

Launch a Noisy, Interactive Exploration for Docking Sites

It can be hard for a genuine entrepreneurial type to pull back on this exploring phase of things. It's in the blood, I think. So, there's good in knowing when to stop and declare the portfolio and the target docking sites are of sufficient variety. Bear in mind that all these processes are iterative. A good way of describing this is *diverge with noisy exploration, converge for focus and targeting.*

> *Diverge with Noisy Exploration, Converge for Focus on Docking Sites Found*

For the entrepreneur at heart these iterations of diverging/converging can be exciting. When to converge? No real answer. Let your intuition aided by feedback (and sometimes blowback) guide you.

Learning on the cheap

The *orthodox* next step is to approach a funding group—usually an angel investor—who takes a stake in your promising startup. Since the aim here is a Lean Startup with you maintaining control, let's defer on that.

If your offers are well articulated, you might first go to a procurement office in a relevant business and share them. Alas, procurement doesn't buy innovation—which is what you are trying to sell. Typically, the procurement office wants to see product specs, pricing charts, client references, etc. Much too soon for a Lean Startup.

However, there are people in these relevant businesses who are excellent sources of information for the products and services they need. These are the line managers, the back-office people, even the executives who are not in the position to buy directly from you. But they are the ultimate buyers, with procurement acting on their behalf. They are the ones to talk to.

That is what I did.

I set out very simply to hobnob with these people, to get to know them. They can be found everywhere. At industry conferences—where they are the most open to talking. In associations from the Kiwanis and Lions clubs to industry-specific groups—

where they are more relaxed among kindred spirits. At charity group functions—where their hearts are open and deep relationships over shared concerns are naturally forged. On LinkedIn and industry forums—where they are busy promoting themselves and learning more about their fields of interest.

You want to engage with them as naturally as possible, of course. And in doing so you want to bring the *vocabulary* that you build up around your portfolio of offers. You are looking to crisp this vocabulary in every conversation, making it more easily understandable and resonant with your audiences.

As these interactions happen over the weeks and months, several things emerge.

You learn of the business needs and pain points that your prospects are wrestling with so that you may be able to untangle or satisfy them in the near future. You learn of your prospect's own personal aspirations. It is the individual desires, ambitions, and hidden hopes that mean the most to every one of us. That's what drives real demand.

Advertising execs know this. They know that aspirations trigger needs, which trigger demand, so they try to gin up aspiration in us. That is the startup's goal as well—to be sought in every interaction.

This is the seeding phase of business, interacting with people who could become customers, *socializing* your ideas, getting feedback on them, *blending* and *iterating* toward a stronger and stronger set of offers.

Seed Relevant Communities with Increasingly Refined Offers

When these offers map nicely to your target audience's corporate needs as well as personal aspirations, it is time to take them formally to potential customers by finding and targeting *docking sites*.

For me, this happened in the fall of 1982. It felt Dickensian—for it was a yeasty time to be in technology, but the overall economy was moribund.

On the "best of times" side of the ledger there were big happenings in technology. We were on the precipice of a new computing revolution with IBM having introduced the personal computer and Apple already making waves with its portable ones.

As for the "worst of times," you had a country deep into a terrible economic downturn. One in ten people couldn't find jobs. Inflation was well above 10 percent and the home mortgage rates had exceeded 15 percent. Businesses faced plummeting sales and thought only of cutting costs. If open to hearing about anything, it was about offers that could demonstrably cut costs or drive improved productivity gains.

Into this milieu I inexpertly tried to launch.

Reality check: Facing the likelihood of failure

The Census Bureau tells us that some five million new business applications are filed every year now, up nearly 100 percent from a decade ago.[5]

Statista tells us that less than one million companies are one year or less old.[6] So roughly one out of five make it through the first year.

This winnowing only becomes more brutal. In 2022, there were about two hundred IPOs, which is close to the average.[7] This means that about one in twenty-five thousand startups makes it all the way to a Rich Exit.

Tracking these Rich Exits even further and looking out beyond the IPO a few years, more than half are underwater.[8] They are either losing money or underperforming compared to initial expectations.

This alarming news has actually gotten worse in recent years, throttling down America's great engine of capitalism.

Back in the mid-1990s, there were 7,322 companies listed on major US stock exchanges and the US population was 266 million.[9] That means there were about twenty-eight listed companies for every million citizens. That was the peak. By 2023, the number of public companies dropped to 5,860 while the population hit 332 million. That works out to about eighteen companies per million. So despite three decades of feverish-paced IPOs, public companies are being lost.

Beyond IPOs, how have rich acquisitions like Kenan Systems fared?

In the last decade, the number of US deals has run between ten thousand and fourteen thousand per year, with total deal value of around $2 trillion.[10] The value distribution can skew year to year because of megadeals—such as the 2021 acquisition of Kansas City Southern by Canadian Pacific Railway for $33.6 billion, creating the first rail network from Canada into Mexico.[11] But if we narrow in on these M&A stats, looking at Rich Exits totaling $1 billion or more, we find that on average ten startups a year make it to that fabled unicorn status.[12] This information is sourced from a Harvard Business School study in 2020 that looked at startups in business less than twenty years. So these were companies that put a business model to work and delivered on it in a relatively short period of time.

Thus we find that beginning with five million new startups every year, about ten will go on to become unicorns via an IPO or acquisition—one in five hundred thousand.

Most of these companies that do achieve a Rich Exit are VC backed, and the number of Lean Startups without VC funding that make it to a Rich Exit shrinks down easily by half (yes, one in a million!).

If you have entrepreneurial blood coursing through your veins, you don't see one in a million as an obstacle but instead a challenge. So onward ...

Don the Armor of Ambiguity, and Plunge In

There's going to be great uncertainty front-loaded into any business venture, more so with a startup—ambiguity and uncertainty as far as the eye can see. And only one way to stand up to it all: start defying the numbers stacked against you

First, for a little proof in the pudding

Since we're talking about the principles of startup success, it's fair to ask right up front about the proofs for my principles and framework for success. Actually, I have the most delightful proof elements—because they are deeply personal.

My older son, Kent Sahin, went to work for CMD after college and continued on with Lucent after the acquisition until 2001, all along a first-rate student and practitioner of the CMD culture and principles.

In 2003 he started his own company with a software platform he acquired, though admittedly needing more than $1,000 startup capital. He did, however, remain private and took no outside capital or debt. Using the tenets of CMD, which he enhanced and perfected over fifteen years, he turned his company *REAL Software Systems* into an international leader in intellectual property (IP) rights management in seven different industries including pharma, studios, publishing, software, and gaming, using a common platform and building blocks. His customers included Microsoft, IBM, MGM, Disney, Getty, Activision, Hasbro, the BBC, Cambridge University Press, and another eighty companies of that caliber. And much like I did, he negotiated every single contract using the principles we're looking at here.

Kent was headed toward an astronomical valuation in another five years or so comparable to KSC, but he chose family instead. He sold his company as the sole shareholder for a still substantial amount, a Rich Exit leaving him time with his delightful wife and three young children. The grandpa in me considered it the richest of exits.

A second proof point is what I started "accidentally"—TIAX (more on this in chapter 9). It was a startup of a different sort—taking over the lab-based division (Technology and Innovation) of the fabled Arthur D. Little, Inc., which after 116 years of operations was liquidated in an auction in Boston in 2002. TIAX launched with 250 people hired overnight, operating over ninety labs. Without any layoffs or salary cuts, TIAX became a prospering business, leading to the creation of CAMX Power, which is even more successful. In both cases, I used many of the principles I describe in this book.

Launching like an oddball into business

Since I launched CMD in a Dickensian time I chose to keep focused on the "best of" aspect of things. Because we were on the precipice of a computing revolution, and we could see how the ones and zeroes could line up in new digital solutions. It was like having a big fermenting pot of wealth on the stove with lots of cheerleaders, and even more doubters and critics weighing in from all sides.

I am reminded of an old Hodja story. Hodja was a wise man who lived in thirteenth-century Turkey—lesser known in the West than Aesop, but he too had a fable for every situation. There was Hodja busily dumping a bucket of yogurt into a pond, passersby asking, "Why, Hodja, are you crazy?" He responds, "As you can see, I am trying to turn it into a pond of yogurt." Everyone laughed at him, ridiculed him.

Today we see twenty-first-century breakthroughs completing Hodja's effort for us. What if the new CRISPR-9 technologies can edit new genes into bacteria living in the pond so that organic detritus like dead leaves and insects can be digested by the bacteria and turned into something roughly approximating, yes, milk?

Hodja was not far off tossing yogurt with its lactobacillus into the pond to do whatever bacteria do to create a pond of yogurt. If Hodja the entrepreneur ignored the doubters and had gone ahead and patented his discovery, he could have become a dominant player in the yogurt industry and maybe in the cheese industry, as well.

At CMD I was throwing that proverbial bacillus into the pond, trying to figure out the future on the fly, with no shortage of doubters. So I continued working on the first principles of my company, wrapping a *vocabulary* around the ideas I hoped would resonate with potential clients and the team I'd soon be hiring.

One of those first principles derived from watching the steady stream of students coming to MIT over the years. Watching them struggle mightily at first with the workload, trying not to buckle under the academic rigor, finding that the first step every semester was the hardest, then finding that it didn't get any easier if genuine mastery was the student's goal, only then realizing what a satisfying journey it had been.

It was that student journey that inspired some of CMD's earliest vocabulary out in the business world ...

The First Step Is 80% of the Way There, But So Is the Last Step and So Are the Middle Steps

Along with …

Difficulties Do Not Go Away, But You Do Get Better at Handling Them

2

INITIAL CLIENTS, NOW WHAT?

Acquiring the first customers

No customers, no business, no validation. And so I began an extensive outreach program to my network of contacts. I phoned prospects to request in-person meetings. I sent lengthy letters to them. Several months went by with zero responses.

Finally, a callback came from Jerry Lee. He was the equivalent of a senior VP at the USPS.

What a way to start!

We had an excellent meeting, since Jerry had a very large number of potential *docking sites*. He described a particularly difficult issue that he thought could benefit from an analytical framework CMD could provide. He needed to approve a major acquisition using either a purchase or lease strategy and, given the rapidly rising interest rates at the time, he was facing a difficult decision. I outlined the analytical framework for the problem and in the same meeting engaged in some *noisy exploration*, seeding the conversation with several *offers* in the CMD *portfolio*.

He decided to move forward, and CMD was in business! I was led to the contracting officer to make it official.

Since it was a small commission, it didn't require the usual competitive bidding. And within a week or so, it was completed to Jerry's satisfaction. More importantly, many seeds were planted and now Jerry knew that CMD could deliver a wide array of software-based offers. I could expect more projects, and larger projects, sprouting up in the years to come.

I had worked up a *portfolio of offers*, interacted with potential customers, *socialized* ideas with them, *blended* various ideas, seeded for the future, iterated toward a workable solution, won a small starter project, interacted some more, and seeded some more. All of these steps had come together in a single sustainable, go-to-market strategy summarized as …

> *Find an Entry Point and Radiate into Unexpected Opportunities*

And Citibank makes two

My second callback, making it possible to now draw at least a feeble trendline for my upstart startup, came from Carlos Salvatori at Citibank's Institutional Banking unit. Soon we met. Carlos listened attentively to my pontifications about …

- Ways to uncover hidden insights in Citibank's customer base using new ideas we were calling Big Data and multidimensional data modeling.

- Ways to boost the productivity of Citibank's complex financial systems using the Expert Systems and Natural Language Processing that I'd worked on for medical diagnoses back in 1977 when I was a visiting professor at MIT's computer science department. (There I'd collaborated with Professors Peter Szolovits and Michael Dertousos, the latter who brought Dr. Tim Berners-Lee to MIT. This augmented group spearheaded Web 2.0, which then helped the emergence of the likes of Amazon, Google, etc.)

- Ways that repetitive back-office tasks could be handled using AI production rules, basically transforming the knowledge book stored in the heads of bank clerks into a set of rules for getting repetitive jobs done superfast.

When finally I took a breath, Carlos thanked me for my time and said, "Good luck with all your ideas." I can still recall his words and tone.

Weeks passed by. I figured, oh well, at least I'd given it my best shot. And then the phone rang.

Carlos was wondering if those expert systems I'd described could be used to automate the funds transfer messages that Citibank was manually processing in huge quantities.

Apparently, the seed I'd planted finally sprouted. That happened, I soon learned, because Carlos's boss wanted Citibank to improve this laborious task. All of a sudden Citibank's corporate needs and Carlos's own aspirations were in alignment. My *vocabulary* now fully resonated ...

- Having repetitive tasks

- Needing well-articulated rules

- Handling high volumes

- Keeping people in the loop

And there it was—part of the formula was emerging.

Having embedded a *vocabulary* in the prospect's mind …

Having shown in fairly understandable terms how we could meet his real-world pain points and aspirations …

Having done this within the context of both personal and corporate objectives and business drivers …

Our little company ended up landing a very exciting project.

Just as in the USPS case, we were able to radiate out and later land other projects with Citibank.

It's worth amplifying this first principle of *radiating*.

It's obviously essential that you come prepared with *target topics* selected from your *portfolio of offers* to talk about in a prospecting meeting using good descriptors or *vocabulary*. A well-crafted vocabulary set (lexicon) around your offers is like formulas in math and science. Complex ideas neatly packaged in just a few lines of symbols.

It's also important to introduce some side topics—that is, *noise*. I even wrote a short paper as a professor on "Noise as an Organizer." The key notion was that adding random variability, or noise, opens up new pathways for engagement, exploration, discovery, and getting past blockages. I saw it applying to many aspects of life. It was Darwin who argued that chance or random genetic mutations, i.e., noise, would cause a particular phenotype—such as height, eye color, or blood type—to be more favorable to its environment and thus drive evolution via natural selection. This concept of noise is now widely used, including in and by generative AI. I used it extensively. In my presentations to executives at Citibank, USPS, and later at other companies and forums, I would lead with a crisp presentation of my top topics. But I would keep alert for opportunities to segue into some noisy digression that could expand the discussion, open up a new line of thought, and perhaps even pop open a new opportunity at some later date. I was never afraid to try something new. And then having digressed, I would make certain to return to the top topics quickly enough to keep the conversation flowing, iterative diverge/converge.

This concept of *noise* is fully operationalized in the consumer products world. We go to the supermarket to buy a toothbrush and end up with a basketful of goods, perhaps even forgetting the toothbrush. If the store sold only toothbrushes, that's all we'd buy. No noise, no digressions, no extra purchases, maybe no purchases at all.

We'll return to the Citibank experience in chapter 3 and talk about a core learning that can be critical to success.

A tiny company partnering with the giants

Jerry Lee from USPS called again in 1983 with an unusual request. The Assistant Postmaster General (the equivalent of an executive VP) supporting the Postmaster General (PMG, the equivalent of a CEO) wanted to take a key paper report meant for only the PMG and transform it into a digital format. And he wanted it done fast because the report's author was retiring in four months. I hopped on the next flight to Washington.

Now this may seem like an easy task. But recall the 1980s. People were still waiting until after 7 p.m. to make off-peak-rate phone calls. Dial-up modems were state of the art. Portable computers were brand new. And most relevantly, the Postal Service was massively complex, stretched out discontinuously across the States. It was quasi-privatized and entirely responsible for generating its revenue to meet its expenses (no taxpayer money or subsidies), but the postal rates had to be approved by a quasi-government board, the Postal Rate Commission. In that context, the Postal Service budget had to be submitted to the Commission and Congress.

Still, I thought I could handle it without a hitch.

Next stop, the USPS contracting office. We began drawing up a sole-source contract for $50,000 with the justification provided by the headquarters. That alone should have made me suspicious, but it did not. I was still the naïve academic, and $50,000 was more than my professor's salary!

The contracting officer asked for my hourly rate. Since it was a government contract, I thought $50 per hour sounded about right. The officer eyed me a long second and asked, "How do I know you're worth it?"

I reached into my briefcase and produced a standard commercial consulting invoice with $300 per hour. It was a deal-cinching display of comparative pricing's value, I thought proudly to myself, and that it demonstrated to the contracting officer what a bargain my services were.

Only later did I realize how foolish I was.

I had vastly underpriced the contract. Partly learning from this misstep as a newly minted entrepreneur, I came to appreciate how crucial *pricing* is in the success of a startup.

On my first return visit to Washington to map out the project, I learned what exactly this little report to the Postmaster General entailed. It was prepared by ten analysts at the Financial Analysis Branch who took a vast reservoir of financial and payroll systems data and then categorized it all into fourteen cost and revenue segments. It was a massive and astounding work product that needed to be hosted online when it had previously been typed on paper.

OK so far.

But the report also had to be submittable to Congress on a secure basis. It had to be used by the Postmaster General in postal rate requests and labor union negotiations. So, it had to be both efficient and secure and updatable on a moment's notice.

Contract in hand, I rented offices in Cambridge and persuaded six students at the MIT Sloan School to join CMD—hitherto just me, me, and me—on a part-time basis. Steve Dalton, Dave Daniels, Beth Reiland, Barnaby Sheridan, Kurt Silverman, Darren Walsh, and I next set out to do what was then impossible because we didn't know as much.

I began briefing this amazing team and was met with piercing stares. In what alternative world, they wondered, could we accomplish all that was required in just four months and at $50,000? How could I even afford to pay them, never mind all the equipment and so on as well as the rent ...?

They were better educated in business than their professor.

There was a lesson in there for me, I was sure, a lesson I was slow to learn but learn I did eventually: even as the *offer portfolio* is assembled, some rudimentary thinking about *pricing* is important. For the potential customer, if there is interest in an offer, pricing comes up very quickly. No forethought can lead to gross underpricing (which is what happened to me) or overpricing, which could quickly end a potential sales conversation. Getting pricing or at least price ranges right is a critical part of converting offers to orders.

Couple Offers with Rough Price Ranges

Having been taught a thing or two by my freshly hired part-time working students, I hopped back down to Washington to renegotiate the contract. It involved a good deal of pushing and tugging, but I came away with a time and materials contract capped at $250,000.

Much more reasonable. I was beginning to learn the art of negotiations and pricing and feeling good about myself.

Only later did my new friends at the USPS admit that many before me had attempted the task and failed. A big systems and consulting company had been paid several million dollars for it and failed. They were rooting for us, though, but reiterated that the whole thing had to be done in *four* months.

Such is life and its opportunities.

We had a tight timeline, a spare budget, and a handful of part-time staff for mission impossible. We were going to take what we faced as fixed and get going. And we were about to see firsthand the kinds of miracles talent can achieve.

Our approach became a key component of a Lean Startup ...

Achieve More in Less Time with Fewer Resources

It has always been amazing to me how human ingenuity and creativity can combine in the crucible of the early-stage startup to forge an outsized set of accomplishments.

A good example from the 1960s that now seems so distant, so ancient in fact, involved the early days of cybernetics and computer science. I was an undergrad at MIT then, which meant I was one of those nerds carrying around sleeves of punch cards. We worked on a mainframe. It had a total of 8K core memory. To put this in perspective, that's 100× less memory than the app on your cellphone that turns on the little flashlight.

But in that spartan computing environment and its equivalents elsewhere, computing languages were already developed—Fortran, COBOL LISP, which was laying the early foundations for the building of AI-driven solutions to business problems, and XSIM.

So we have intellectual heft behind us

These new programming languages made all the difference in our ability to deliver business solutions as a Lean Startup. We chose the Stratagem programming language to write the USPS software. The precursor to Stratagem, XSIM, was developed at the MIT Department of Economics and then commercialized by another MIT grad. Stratagem was designed to deal with multidimensional dataset needs (i.e., the need to include the date, time, amount, department, location, age, education, and on and on), a forerunner of today's linked spreadsheet apps.

At USPS, we had three audiences: the executives, the analysts, and the IT department maintaining all the data centers and databases that at the time tracked 750,000 employees and a nearly $35 billion annual budget.

Our impossible mission, which we had already accepted, was to link the system we were to develop to these databases and use the analysts' tools and algorithms organized into fourteen cost segments to reduce all this to *information chunks* for the executives to understand and use for their high-level decisions as well as supporting the budget submissions to Congress, rate negotiations with the Rate Commission, and, we learned later, labor negotiations.

These three audiences have their equivalents in most large organizations: the IT department, the end-users or ultimate consumers, and the analysts that come in between.

IT is primarily responsible for systems that collect, sort, store, and maintain data and of course the exercise of those systems to process, organize, and transmit data. The analysts like accountants or financial analysts or HR have their tools and models and algorithms to convert the data coming from IT (also augmented by their own databases) to a variety of data chunks often mapped into spreadsheets and reports, which are then reviewed and further analyzed by the end-users, at which point data becomes information.

In concept, very simple. Data is source-oriented, becomes information when received by the target of the data.

> *Data Is Source-Generated and Only Becomes Information Once Received and Put in Context*

Example: Two people are in conversation. The source sends data in terms of sound waves organized into data chunks—that is, words. It is understood or gains meaning or becomes information only at the receiver end. If the source just makes random sounds, there is no information at the receiving end. If the sender speaks in Chinese but the receiver does not know Chinese, the data is conveyed in words but is not information.

Simple indeed. But this chain was rudely interrupted by what I will call a marketing gimmick in the 1960s. Some clever people in the field relabeled "data processing" as "information technology" or simply IT and the hitherto unglamorous data processing departments became information technology departments—or simply IT.

And the confusion since then has been enormous. To date, the untoward and confusing and often harmful consequences persist.

Data Processing Relabeled as Information Technology Has Led to Continuing Confusion

IT thinks they are vending information. Who can blame them? It says so in the name of their department. Misled by the label, end-users go to IT to get information. In reality, IT vends data, which becomes information only in the context of the end-user experience. How is IT supposed to know the context of the end-users? It's almost impossible. Even if it is known at one point, it keeps changing.

I used to teach these concepts in passing in the classroom. In my field validation that my Lean Startup was to do, I was to discover how central these concepts would be and how we would find ways of converting them to practice and successful outcomes.

To restate, in organizations at least three distinct groups mediate data to information: IT (in realty DP) with their powerful computers, systems, and databases; analysts with their models, algorithms, spreadsheets, local databases, and links to IT; and end-users facing internal and external environments often in flux.

Each of these units has its own needs, demands, requests, culture, viewpoints, environments, tools, task clusters, and emotions.

IT needs deep planning to manage the vast complexity they face. And the systems they maintain need exact specifications embodied in massive documentation. Computers do not tolerate ambiguity. IT needs predictability and precision and is expected to be almost error-free. In thousands of reports generated, heaven forbid if there are a few errors! It is doomsday. Credibility is questioned.

The analysts live in a world of complex algorithms, equations, linked spreadsheets, and scenarios. Their mission is to reduce the vast streams of data from IT into meaningful and manageable chunks with many, many assumptions or constructs, to make all kinds of assessments and predictions and generate many hypotheses. It is OK for the results to be inaccurate, somewhat vague, embedded in many speculative scenarios. Often, scenarios are what drive their world and serve as the syntax.

The analysts, while receiving piles of data from IT, do not necessarily share their algorithms or formulas or spreadsheets with IT. That is one area of darkness or ignorance for IT.

The ultimate end-users live in an environment of ambiguity, uncertainty, and incessant change. Competitors introduce new products, old products go obsolete or malfunction, the Federal Reserve increases rates, inflation surges, recession sets in, there is a cash crunch, key employees leave, lawsuits by or against are filed, and on and on.

In this dynamic ever-changing environment, what was information yesterday is useless today. New datasets need to be conveyed to the analysts who can crank out new assessments, new scenarios, and new predictions and present these to the end-users coherently.

Traditional versus our approach to system development

How do you develop an *information system* that will serve the end-users who are after all the internal clients who also pay for the process? And who should do it? Not end-users, as they are the END-users. Not the analysts, as they don't have the deep access to databases and systems that are needed. Naturally, IT. After all, the label on their department says Information Technology.

And how does IT go about it? They develop systems with detailed specifications. They start with a comprehensive plan with Gantt charts, PERT diagrams, milestones, division of work, language choices, and the like all fed into a system architecture. Then they interact with the end-users by having them articulate their needs. After many such meetings followed by many internal meetings in the IT department, *system specifications* are developed. And then begins the programming. The traditional language in the past was COBOL or COmmon Business-Oriented Language. Many systems in companies are still coded in COBOL.

All this sounds logical. But coming at it from my experiences in academia and teaching the Sloan Fellows, the process seemed highly flawed. If nothing else, the time that such an approach takes—often years—can render them obsolete on arrival.

Another big flaw: when end-users are asked what they will need, of course, they will go for the sky. Why not? There is no risk in asking and best to cover all bets. But for IT, the consequences of such open-ended user-need identification are huge. It leads to systems being bloated and then delayed and then slow to run.

In my interactions with the Sloan Fellows and experiences in the field, I could see that these three groups often do not necessarily respect or trust each other.

End-users thought then (and many still do) that IT really does not understand their needs, they always want more time, more money, and they are still late.

IT thinks the end-users are not cognizant of the complexities in going from "wants" to the system equivalents of those wants. Worse, end-users cannot even articulate what they want in cogent narratives.

If IT, heaven forbid, has a single error in many pages, the end-users are quick to criticize. But it is OK for end-users to send to IT ambiguous memos even with many spelling or grammatical errors.

Differences over time often lead to the siloing of projects, which results in further mistrust and suspicion or even contempt for each other.

At CMD, we faced another challenge: being the outsiders (automatically suspect) we had to mediate the three distinct silos to create new and superfast data streams if were to get done in four months.

As an academic, I was quite used to multiple and at times clashing cultures. The undergraduate needs and culture are quite different from those of graduate students in the master's programs in science and engineering, which differ from those in MBA programs. And the PhD students are altogether in a different world. Then there is the faculty and, of course, the administration. Academics typically have to make do with spartan resources. Only a few of them have dedicated secretaries or assistants and the rest have to share one such person for many.

Result: an academic has to wear many hats or have many faces or many personas. She has to smoothly navigate among many audiences or clients each within their own mini worlds.

So, it became clear that faced with the challenges of what turned out to be redesigning a whole budget system for USPS in a mere four months with but a team of seven part-timers (me being the seventh as I was still on the faculty), I had to practice the multifaceted persona that I had honed through the years but also train my team.

Trainable they were, as they had not been yet shaped by years of experience and specialization. (Later I was to discover the power of this trainability that stemmed from naïveté and lack of experience and actually made it a cornerstone of my hiring.)

Part of the training is creating descriptors or vocabulary. I coined *splitsuit*. We would appear before the end-users in our suits and talk in business terms. We had that background, anyway. We could converse on financial or HR or production decisions the client was facing and understand their world in their terms.

For the analysts, we would go in dressed as nerds, easily conversing in spreadsheets, debits and credits, simulation models, and net present value analysis.

And when we met with IT, we might even be wearing blue jeans and tie-dyed shirts, somewhat disheveled, looking like systems hacks or system engineers. And our world to them was bits and bytes, relational databases, debugging, subroutines, etc.

Same team, different attire, different terms, perceived as different people altogether. Splitsuits. The impact was great and led to us being trusted by each unit. And without trust, real communication can be tough.

To the executives, we were anchoring our systems in a business use case they understood. To IT, we were laying out well-documented systems and then retreating as fast as possible, allowing the systems to be stitched in at both ends.

A corny analogy is Superman: dressed in ordinary clothes, a shy awkward guy. Sheds his suit and he is Superman. We were not quite Superman but to several of our clients we became miracle workers. A single team of seven seemed like a big army of specialist teams.

> *Practice Splitsuit Interactions to Speak the Language of Each Corporate Audience*

When we executed this splitsuit strategy well, our delivered system would (a) be internalized by each unit and (b) successfully bridge the great yawning chasms that so often separated IT, the analysts, and end-using executives.

Having thus found ways of reaching each audience on their own terms, I had to decide where to begin and how to begin. An experience I had years earlier learned rather dramatically in my early days of teaching became my guidepost.

Together with a colleague, Avery Johnson, who had a PhD in cybernetics, we introduced a course, "Self-Organizing Systems." It was a sellout.

To celebrate, we went to a high-end restaurant on his dime, since I was still the broke academic and he was independently wealthy. When the black-tied waiter presented the menu, Avery asked to be taken to the kitchen, explaining to the clearly annoyed waiter that he, Avery, had no trust in the *descriptions* on the menu. He wanted to see *embodiments* in the kitchen, and to chat with the chef. I was frozen, truly embarrassed.

Well, the waiter did reluctantly oblige.

And when Avery returned from the kitchen, he shared a rich bounty of information he'd collected, how some of the menu descriptions were bunk, nothing more than fancy labels for ordinary ingredients, and so on. We put in our orders, and my initial embarrassment was put to rest with a thoroughly excellent meal guided by Avery's firsthand knowledge.

That dinner became a little case study in the difficulty of making a good choice until an *embodiment* is worked up. There is a way to get to such a starting point ...

All New Systems Should Be Rapidly Prototyped

Rapid prototyping is an excellent way to help end-users understand their own thinking, so they can better describe what they really want.

Through rapid prototyping, a robust *functional description* can be developed in weeks as opposed to system specs that can take forever and are often based on end-user expressions of need, which even the end-users are uncertain about.

Uncertain, that is, unless they see embodiments. But how best to create these embodiments? It's not by developing specs. Instead go for descriptions of what functionality the end-users want. People are much more comfortable with descriptions of what they want rather than specifying precisely what they want.

For instance, it is easy to describe a chair: something often with three to four legs, a seat, and often a back. But specifying a chair, that could be a doctoral thesis. If a table is pushed against a wall and I sit on it, does it become a chair and included in the specs?

In efficient conversations in our nicely pressed suits with matching ties, we would interact with the end-users, capturing in descriptive terms the functionalities they were seeking.

We used *models* as the vocabulary to interact with the analysts. Model is a generic term that can encompass formulas, spreadsheets, simulations, accounting rules or constructs, and so on, all in the "kitchen" of the analysts.

The combination of functionality descriptors and models then became the first draft of a *functional description document.* Quick and simple.

Capture What the End-Users Want with a Functional Description

With this functional description in hand, we could quickly create embodiments using rapid prototyping so that the end-users could see what they had described in their terms. It was now easier for them to assess if what they saw was what they had in mind. And if it wasn't, they could concretely come up with pointed requests for change. Then onto the next iteration of the rapid prototype.

Stratagem as a high-level language was ideal for rapid proto-typing USPS's system, which we dubbed *CABS (Computer Analysis and Budgeting System)*. We could go from an initial set of functional descriptions to understandable reports based on simulated data in weeks, even days, and then go back to the end-users while the project scope was still fresh in their minds.

Within a month, we already had many *iterations* of a *rapid prototype to embodiments to a revised prototype.*

The entire skeleton of the system that emerged to achieve the overall function could be tightly summarized

DATA in Networks of Databases Maintained by IT Linked to MODELS Developed by ANALYSTS which Convert DATA to PROTO-INFORMATION Chunks Received by END-USERS Who Put Them into CONTEXTS, which Makes Them INFORMATION

The iterations of rapid prototyping to embodiments to revised prototyping truly empower the end-users and make them the real clients, the architects of the systems they want and will use. A vocabulary for this: end-user-driven system development.

With the system prototyped, the end-user interface came together quickly. In those days, it was called an Executive Information System (EIS). Even though the technology was in its infancy, we were able to develop a Graphical User Interface (GUI) to make life easier for the end-users.

And it meant our summer of 1983 was spent finalizing the architecture of the CABS system for USPS and prepping to link it into USPS's data centers. The largest of those centers was in Raleigh, North Carolina. That would be our first stop.

Getting busted for the first time

Two of us from CMD, myself and a subsequent part-time hire from Sloan, Eric Wilde, arrived at USPS's Raleigh Data Center at the start of a shift, as it happened, and joined hundreds of employees streaming into the cavernous building.

We found the gentleman in charge of financial data. He was competent and helpful but needed to refer us to a colleague across the building. So out into the corridor we went, asking for directions. One woman, puzzled, asked who we were.

Contractors, of course, we told her.

She led us down the hall to … security. A towering crew-cut boulder of a man, as if right out of the movies—red cheeks, perpetual frown, and all—immediately laid into us. "How did *you* get into *this* building?" he barked.

Our having used the employee entrance was unacceptable to him. That we were not wearing employee badges, rather obvious all along, was differently unacceptable. The grilling went on and on, we soon learned, because a bigwig from HQ was on-site and the two of us represented something of a security breach. I thought we were headed to the hoosegow. Frozen, I couldn't think of a way out.

At that very moment, the executive in charge of our project happened to walk by security's open door. He was the visiting bigwig. When he saw my pleading eyes, he rushed in to vouch for us. Our security sergeant's growl turned into a frozen smile.

In the academic world, which relishes openness, you could walk onto any campus and slip into most classrooms. That is appropriate for that ecosystem and should remain so. But the industrial world had very different security requirements, understandably.

As for USPS on that humid Raleigh day, we applied for contractor badges and underwent a thorough vetting by Postal Inspectors (federal agents empowered to make arrests, a point duly noted!).

Somehow, we passed scrutiny after our initial mishap, and had the run of the facility. Little did I know that far more serious wrongdoing lay ahead. It began when one of our team members detected someone *sniffing* our system—trying to download our code.

Victims of corporate espionage

Even in those early days, our crackerjack team had learned the deep processes required to detect intrusions. They identified the sniffer as the employee of the other contractor whose multimillion-dollar contract had been canceled for nonperformance. Most likely, they were looking for an angle back into the contract. And most certainly, they were not happy with some upstart getting the job done in four months and for a small fraction of their expenditure.

I immediately phoned USPS headquarters and supplied the details. We were told the Postal Inspectors would take it from there.

Later we learned that all access privileges for that contractor had been canceled. We were OK, or so we thought.

To move the USPS implementation along, I had asked USPS to give us access codes to various systems so our team could test things. Apparently, the codes we received were temporary ones—somehow that detail escaped my attention.

One day while visiting Jerry Lee in Washington, I was suddenly flanked by two tall FBI types, each grabbing an arm. I was told to follow them. Jerry tried to intervene, but they ignored him.

I was led to a small interrogation room and asked to sit on a metal chair at a desk—just like a criminal suspect. These two Postal Inspectors began raking me over the coals.

As it turned out, when we'd reported the breach of our system, we triggered a comprehensive review. Postal Inspectors found out that we had failed to get our temporary passcodes reauthorized.

They didn't care who I was or what I was doing with USPS; this was unacceptable. I had to be arrested.

It took a long chat, with me constantly reminding the Inspectors that it was I who'd reported the other breach before they relented and *almost* thanked me for my service. A new set of passcodes was authorized. It was one scary experience, and though it ended well, it would be weeks before I slept soundly!

Crafting a knowledge-based company

We learned a lot about taking on impossible challenges with our skeleton crew. With only seven of us crammed into our six-hundred-square-foot office at 238 Main Street in Cambridge, the issue of "who does what" bubbled up early. Tight spaces tend to bring out all kinds of emotions in people! We all had our skillsets and we tried to leverage those intelligently across the workload. But with all seven of us on steep learning curves, each curve a little different, I had to port in a tenet from my teaching days, and it soon became invaluable.

In teaching, I knew that there is never any shame in not knowing something, only in pretending to know and making no effort to close the knowledge gap. This notion is central to the academic experience and yet in short supply in industry, where the focus is on "making it, selling it, and delivering it." So I introduced what I called *Teach & Learn, Learn & Teach* to turn our everyday business activities into a constant teaching of each other and learning from each other's experiences ...

> *Suffuse the Organization with a "Teach & Learn, Learn & Teach" Mindset*

Going hand in hand with this practice is something I called *socializing and blending*—a practice that involved the blending of a team's ideas, criticisms, and alternative suggestions from the very start in order to emerge with a richer idea or decision—what has come to be known as group ideation. This I had learned way back in one of my Sloan Fellow classes when startled by a fellow declaring what I said was crap, as I chronicled earlier.

This can be a risky approach if handled clumsily.

That's because any time an unformed idea is identified as such and then tossed to a group to kick around and consider, someone in the room will nonetheless consider it a *fait accompli* and start acting accordingly, especially if the president starts it. It becomes like the party whisper game. Even worse, actually, because organization communications move not in a linear way around the party circle, but along strings of networked nodes. So, by the time the proposed idea runs the office, it could easily have distorted into gossip and then into misunderstandings and finally into hurt feelings, or worse—misguided actions.

So, you have to be clear from the outset that the idea is just that, an idea.

You have to repeatedly remind people that the socializing and blending of ideas is key to the organization's success, and that there are no locks these keys cannot open.

This reminder would seem almost unnecessary—people should get it, right?

No. This approach is so different from how many top-down organizations work that constant reminding is required until the idea is fully integrated into the company culture and daily communications streams, evolving into trust.

Despite these risks, it is worth it.

It is so enabling to a Lean Startup, it is one of the first principles …

Socializing and Blending Ideas Leads to Better Decision Outcomes

Along with …

Make Sure It Is Always Safe for the Team to Express Their Views

This principle led to a corollary learning again derived from my time teaching the Sloan Fellows.

Our classes drew in an assortment of professions, including doctors moving into managerial positions and seeking the tools, mechanics, and theories of management.

For exams, it had been my practice to allow open books and four-page cheat sheets. It motivated students to know where the answers could be found in the books and to cram summaries in tiny script onto those cheat sheets—compact summary sheets for life.

During one such exam, I was absorbed in a book. Abruptly the room fell quiet. Looking up, I could see all eyes on me. Out along my periphery I had seen a Sloan Fellow rise and approach me. But now I realized the Fellow had disappeared. Turning around, I saw him face down on the floor, making gurgling sounds. In near panic, I turned to the Sloan Fellow I knew to be a doctor, begging for his help.

But he wouldn't move until I asked him to.

I was the authority, and since I was also giving an exam, I had the power. I lurched toward the supine Fellow together with the "student" now acting as the doctor. Together, we revived the Fellow.

Critical learning came out of that day.

A time will come when leadership needs to be transferred to another more qualified. And it will only happen when individuals in the organization are empowered—either implicitly or explicitly.

It may not seem like a big principle, until it is.

Empower the Team to Practice Situational Leadership

When there is a project, someone on the team must take a leadership role and become a "transient boss" or "situational leader" with the rest of the team in subordinate roles. However, when this project is completed, the "transient boss" needs to let go of the reins and hand them over to the next situational leader.

This is not always easy to do. Power is alluring, seductive, and sticky. But if these transitions are not handled smoothly, the workload of the company can suffer.

A beneficial by-product of *situational leadership* is that it leads to stepping into new roles, into the shoes of others, which inevitably enhances learning, thus making *Teach & Learn, Learn & Teach* so much more effective.

For CMD at the time, I fully participated in knowledge engineering and in system architecture development, but not in coding. I became the situational leader, and the doer, as well, for the all-important documentation of our systems and software.

I would furiously crank out documentation drafts on an early PC (known as the *Superbrain*) with its integrated keyboard, 4 MHz processor, and 5" floppy discs. It was the bomb in 1983! I'd send those drafts to our USPS contacts for feedback and make revisions accordingly.

Again, there were only seven of us on this huge project. If we lost even one of the team, it could be near fatal. But one day Barnaby Sheridan angrily informed me that he was resigning, immediately. He could not, would not, work for a company whose president sent reports to the client containing spelling errors!

Apparently, one of those documentation *drafts* had too many typos. And that didn't sit well with him.

I was dumbfounded. I urgently explained to Barnaby that it was just a draft, sent to an executive I knew well, to be revised anyway, all in the spirit of rapid prototyping, literally. Only after I proposed that he proofread every outgoing report did he relent and remain with us. Phew!

We didn't need a first principle to cover that kerfuffle. But from that day forward, a policy was added. Every memo was reviewed by a second set of eyes. Often several sets.

From my handling of the documentation, I also came to appreciate the vital role it plays in a company's internal structuring. Documentation serves to ...

- Coordinate the many different components of a project,

- Operationalize the dynamic configuration of the organization along with the system being developed,

- Act as a proxy master plan for the project.

With situational leadership, *Teach & Learn, Learn & Teach*, socialization, and idea blending as part of our modus operandi, there was an additional issue: *dealing with me.*

The Founder/CEO Works for the Company and Does Not Own It

This may strike you as, well, wrong.

I was the founder but often was introduced as the owner, and my colleagues viewed me as such. But I had decided from the outset to always correct them. No one can own a company since a company is the people in it, quite literally as the term *company* implies, and people cannot be owned. One can own a financial interest. The founder has one mode of financial ownership, the investors another, and the employees still another. But at the end of the day, I worked for the company.

Reinforcing this notion made the other core aspects of the evolving CMD culture, especially situational leadership, so much more effective and real.

Against all odds, we succeeded

We delivered an operational system to USPS for their entire budgeting system—and USPS budget systems were nearly overnight modernized. In time, this system would go through many iterations and upgrades. Its success led us to *radiate* to new commissions to develop other strategic systems for USPS, with one of them ultimately taken into international markets.

3

TAKING AI INTO THE MARKETPLACE

Sunny days of summer success at USPS soon gave way to the arctic blasts of winter, and all the Shetland wool blankets in our Cambridge offices couldn't soothe away the exhaustion our entire team felt. The USPS project had taken as much out of us as we'd given. Despite the successes we could legitimately claim, we were feeling every shade of gray.

I wasn't sure we could ever replicate the success we'd enjoyed with USPS. We'd spent the money we'd earned and now what?

We had only a young team in a little office, with but a single victory.

Bankers in the modern era

When a call came through from Carlos Salvatori of Citibank, fair to say I was a tad overeager. Carlos wanted to know if the advances we'd made in Expert Systems could be put to work converting the telex or wire transfer messages to the SWIFT format that banks used. I eagerly explained to Carlos that it would be an ideal application because these messages were rules-based, well defined, and involving repetitive activities.

A trifecta.

Carlos then admitted to being "frugal," and $50,000 was all he'd pay for this observably nontrivial project.

Of course, I should have walked right then.

I naïvely accepted and managed to bump the retainer fee a little since the project would need to be written in LISP. Short for LISt Processing, LISP was developed at MIT and elsewhere as a programming language that allowed processing "symbols" the way one processes numbers, critical in the early development of AI.

(I was a student of one of the towering figures of AI, Professor Marvin Minsky, and part of the course was using LISP.)

There were two LISP machine vendors at the time. The better known was Symbolics, but their salesperson was less than accommodating, believing that the Symbolics machines would dominate. The other vendor, Lisp Machines Inc. (LMI), was more approachable and better priced, and their president, Frank Spitznogle, got directly involved. With funds from Citibank, I purchased two machines at $50,000 a pop from LMI—one for our Cambridge office and the other for 111 Wall Street, where Citibank's international banking group was located. Spitznogle and I became close professional friends—a relationship that would years later alter the course of our company.

Carlos told me that the project was so small, he didn't need to take it to legal for a contract. I just had to write up a contract for review by his reports, which I did, stipulating that our company, CMD, would retain all IP rights over our work product, and Citibank would have usage rights. His direct report Jim Reilly found it to be reasonable.

This little draft contract would be a key enabler of the success of our Lean Startup and its evolving into a viable Lean Company, as well …

Contracts Are Key to the Success of a Lean Startup and Becoming a Lean Company

There'll be much more on contracts, but I'm getting ahead of myself.

Early on at any startup, especially a lean one like CMD, each member of the team takes on multiple tasks, and agrees to certain responsibilities based on their skillsets. It happens naturally—with or without an org chart.

But that initial team invariably gets tagged as "founders" and are soon locked into work paths and routines. Then as the company grows, they gain in perceived power and their actions can have an overbearing influence on the now much-larger company—to the point of making or breaking it.

So ideally a Lean Company carefully channels those early members to their evolving subject matter expertise rather than letting the initial power base determine that. This would seem obvious on its face, like a walnut is obviously a walnut. But crack it open under the pressure of a startup's deadlines and commitments, and it can get messy, with the fruit of the nut compromised.

I was fortunate to have cracked this nut in academia and tried hard to stand athwart the typical "founders reign" mindset. I gave people credit but *did not* empower them in areas where they were not adding value simply because they were founders. Every day I looked for ways to crack open a key underlying principle …

Everyone, Including the Founders, Works for the Company

With this as part of the modus operandi, it becomes easier to implement a more fundamental principle:

In Making Decisions, Start with the Company Objectives and Interests

So many startups fall short because the original team holds fast to their original domains. They build staffs and projects and tasks around these domains to perpetuate their power base and wherewithal. Being human with often outsized egos, they figure the company is there to help them succeed rather than the other way around. To paraphrase what President Kennedy famously said—ask not what the company can do for you, but what you can do for the company.

Some companies address this issue by forcing people to rotate into new positions every few years. This solves one problem but leads to another—namely losing relevant domain expertise, especially critical on longer-term projects where continuity is key. Far better to …

- Make these team rotations part of the culture, but do them on an *ad hoc* basis to meet the company's larger needs.

- Make certain this practice applies not just to founders but to those who achieve notable feats—such as being the key architect or coder behind a winning systems installation.

This we did at CMD, and in due time, I wrapped this idea into the kind of principle that could go on a poster in the lunchroom …

No Heroes or Hero Worship

In fact, I would emphasize this by saying that heroes are not welcome. Such a mindset of course makes teamwork all the more acceptable and welcome.

Combinatorial complexity, how do I know thee?

With funded Citibank project in hand, I hired Keith Sawyer, an exceptional talent and cognitive science wizard from MIT. With that came our inaugural site visit to Citibank, our first chance to dig into their funds transfer operation. Our CMD team stepped out onto the sprawling floor of Citibank's Funds Transfer department, intending to do some *noisy exploring.*

We found rather low-paid clerks tackling their task manually. Data entry operators would read and analyze incoming wire transfers and then type the information into a standard ASCII terminal interface. They followed a basic rulebook to translate often slapdash wires teeming with ambiguities into the rigid SWIFT format. It was a slow, tedious, error-prone process.

Citibank's IT department had previously tried to automate this process using keyword analysis. But they discovered that even a simple funds transfer message containing dates, dollar amounts, beneficiaries, and the like could generate millions of combinations that keywords couldn't parse.

For instance, the "date" could be entered on the message as March 31 or 31st of March or 3/31 or 31/3 or 3.31. The dollar amount could be $1,000.00 or USD 1000.00 or US$ 1,000 and no cents, or one thousand US dollars, etc. Each field had all kinds of these variations.

Citibank had stumbled onto the shores of combinatorial complexity. The immense cruelty of this problem is too easily underappreciated. Allow me to explain why …

Consider a light display device that has bulbs arranged in twenty rows and twenty columns of four hundred bulbs, each bulb on or off. It's a rather primitive array. Today displays exceed millions of rows and columns.

Two questions:

How many combinations, or patterns if you will, could meet a single criterion that we decide on?

How long will it take a superfast computer to give us an answer?

I've posed these questions many times to lay and technical audiences, and for fun I've requested that they answer right away.

The first question is easy to answer, mathematically speaking.

For the second question—that is, how long will it take to find a certain pattern in the array using a supercomputer—I've gotten answers ranging from "a few seconds" to "a couple of minutes" with a few outliers guessing a longer time period.

All way off the mark!

The number of unique patterns?

- With one bulb, we have two patterns—on or off.

- With two bulbs, each having two states, there would be 2 × 2 or four patterns.

- For 400 bulbs, there would be 2 × 2 × 2 … or 400 multiples of 2, or 2 to the power of 400. That's written in decimal notation roughly as 10^{120} (or one hundred octovigintillion, for those inclined to wonder). Suffice it to say, it's a large number. Even larger than a googol, 10^{100}, which inspired Google's company name.

Now if we want to find a pattern that fits a particular criterion, whatever it might be, we have to examine each and every one of the patterns, as our answer could come from the first or the last; we cannot be certain until we review them all.

Using superfast computers, how long would it take?

Suppose our computer can look at ten billion or 10^{10} patterns a second—quite fast. So the time required is 10^{120} divided by 10^{10}, which is 10^{110} seconds, roughly 10^{102} years. Sounds like a long time, and it is. Our universe since the Big Bang is thought to be 13.6 billion years old, or roughly 15×10^{10} years. So, if we had started looking for this specified pattern back at the Big Bang, we'd still be not far from the start of our search!

What if we daisy-chained a bunch of superfast computers and set them to the task together? I have posed that question, as well. And the answers I've received to the "how long" question have bumped up only to "hours" and "perhaps months."

Again, not even close.

The known universe is thought to have 10^{80} elementary particles—such as photons and electrons. Suppose each one of these particles was a supercomputer spinning through ten billion patterns a second. Clearly an incredible notion, but good as a thought exercise ...

With every particle in the universe now working for us, our compute rate is 10^{80} particles times 10^{10} patterns processed, or 10^{90} total computing power. Wow! But hold on.

Remember that we have 10^{120} patterns to examine for our little 400×400 bulb array. So the time we'll need is 10^{120} divided by 10^{90}, which is 10^{30} seconds. That's still far greater than the age of the known universe.

In this simple example, we have a search problem that the whole universe acting as a massive set of computers cannot solve. As for us mere mortals?!

Therein lies the cruelty of combinatorial complexity.

No wonder Citibank's attempts at converting wire transfer messages to rigidly formatted SWIFT messages using keywords stumbled.

Taming combinatorial complexity begins with finding ways to simplify the search domain. There are a myriad of approaches.

One powerful approach is "tree pruning." You narrow your focus to the most promising branches of the massive combinatorial tree.

Another approach is "statistical sampling" that is used extensively.

Another is to use "heuristics" or mental shortcuts or rules of thumb.

Combining these approaches is what I call *judicious simplification*. But this simplification is far from enough if the search space is large.

In any complex situation, there will be all kinds of ambiguities. By adding *context*, you can disambiguate or remove more layers of uncertainty. Often there is lingering ambiguity. So you impose a third process I call *ambiguity and uncertainty tolerance*. This is a filter that you adjust based on the context and the objectives for the task. In a funds transfer message, for example, we could be off on the date but not on the dollar amount.

Ultimately our team concluded that we would need to combine Expert Systems with Rule-Based Processing and symbol-syntax-semantics processing that is really Natural Language Processing.

> *To Master Complex Situations, Combine Judicious Simplification with Ambiguity and Uncertainty Tolerance*

Our own Keith Sawyer played a key role in taming Citibank's wire transfer problem. Keith had been something of an iconoclast from the start, showing up for his initial interview at CMD with paint splashes on his pants and later surrounding his desk with pillows for "doing my thinking." Keith was also an engineering, coding, and typing phenom, banging out our initial twenty-five-page Citibank knowledge engineering document from memory with nearly zero errors.

(Keith is today an Endowed Distinguished Professor at UNC, Chapel Hill and the author of eleven books on creativity and innovation.[13] In a recent letter, he shared with me that many of his root ideas were learned at or inspired by CMD.)

Keith, the team, and I conceived of "meaning islands" connected with "syntax bridges," a form of Natural Language Processing. Keith and the team started coding our approach in LISP, and a couple of months later, we presented our solution, which we named CitiExpert. We had set out to solve a problem thought unsolvable via conventional approaches, and our solution was an unqualified success. Icing on the cake was CitiExpert receiving the bank chairman's annual technology award.

Keith and I went on to publish our groundbreaking work in the 1989 Proceedings of the First International Congress on AI. Our commercial success with Expert Systems and Natural Language Processing took AI to a whole new level of implementation in industry.

The semantic parsing of meaning from text using our Natural Language Processing was so far ahead of its time, the US intelligence organization MITRE wanted to use it for classified work. We turned the request away.

Despite pulling off the "mission impossible" for Citibank, we were reminded soon after the project's completion that we were dealing with big business.

Rejecting the "Big IP Lie"

With CitiExpert now one of Citibank's mission-critical systems, the bank's head of IT demanded that I turn over all IP rights as well as the platform code.

I kindly refused.

So, I was summoned to HQ to face the music from a high-powered New York lawyer who fancied having his initials sewn into every article of clothing he was wearing, in gold thread of course. Even before I cleared the threshold, he was barking at me, "Dr. Sahin, you don't understand. We paid for it; therefore, it is ours." What's more, he added, "I don't have time to waste on such a mundane matter."

I responded that I rather liked his fancy shirt.

That sent him into visible anger, and I was berated for being so frivolous.

I informed him that to the contrary, I was quite serious. I really did like his shirt and was curious as to whether he had paid for it.

Too dumbfounded to even be wary, he said yes of course he paid for it.

So I said, "Since you paid for it, surely you must own the pattern IP rights."

He looked puzzled.

Then I let it rip: "Sir, please don't tell this naïve academic that when you pay for something you automatically acquire the IP. When you buy a car, as a second example, GM still owns the IP. As a lawyer, you should know that ownership is based on contracts and my contract with Citibank says we own it. If you want to have it, I will sell it to you. But why would you want that? You have all the usage rights you need."

That put an end to the lawyer's charade.

We retained IP ownership rights for CitiExpert and all the systems that followed. And we won one for the little guy—ourselves, in that instance. But the legal claim that "we paid for it; therefore, it is ours" is a lie that can crush the prospects of a small company.

Holding on to IP when doing work for hire is no easy task because the false dogma of "we paid for it; therefore, it is ours" is just as deeply entrenched in business today as it was in the 1980s.

No matter which law school they attend, every business lawyer in the making goes to the same "finishing school" where they learn *The Great IP Lie*. It's a seven-word mantra taught to flow mellifluously off their lips …

"We paid for it; therefore, we own it."

On the surface, this concept appears to make sense and many entrepreneurs simply accept it. Startups feeling pinched and needing to generate revenue, even if that means entering into less-than-favorable contracts, often succumb.

Big companies know it.

These big companies enter into a multitude of contracts for goods and services. They naturally, and by that I mean aggressively, push for all they can get. Often this means reaching well beyond what they are actually paying for.

These companies want to view these goods and services as "commissioned" or "works for hire." And this is the time when *The Great IP Lie* card is played.

This is also the time to push back and negotiate. *Truth is, payment entitles one to a bundle of rights. What those rights are is a matter of negotiation and mutual agreement.*

For example, paying for a hotel room for a night entitles one to stay there one night—that is all. Leasing a house for a month is just that—there is no ownership automatically granted.

Then there is car buying. No IP ownership comes with the title to the car. Or if it is a lease, the rights are capped (e.g., to miles, to a time period). Full ownership is not automatically granted.

Many entrepreneurs who push back on *The Great IP Lie* find the big company's fallback position is to propose a compromise: joint ownership. Even that can become a future obstacle while unnecessarily diluting the valuation of the startup.

As CMD grew, I ended up negotiating hundreds of contracts and encountered *The Great IP Lie* ad nauseum. I would tell the fancy shirt story many times, and usually win. But not always.

To achieve an overall winning record, I had to lay other supportive arguments on the table.

When is financing not financing?

Once, the big-company lawyer completely refused to budge. They were paying for it, they owned it, end of discussion.

I pointed out that they were just financing the project since there were all kinds of contingencies along the way with milestone payments, decisions, etc., which meant with all these strings attached to progress payments I was bearing ongoing risks. So instead of them "financing" the project, why not wait until the end and decide then if they wanted to buy the deliverables—like a purchase transaction?

He was confused by this but had to go along. At project end, we sold them usage rights only. After having made this argument, if one accepts payment, its financing nature becomes clear and shifts the ground for negotiation, as there are many competing sources of financing, including banks.

When is owning IP not worth it?

Another approach is to point out the inherent costs/risks of IP ownership.

Should a third party want to commission a project based on the original IP, or ask for an adaptation or customization of the existing platform, or be interested in developing derivative products ... then owning any resultant IP means responsibility for any infringements.

Indeed, if another entity infringes, or outright steals the IP, the owner of the IP must then sue, or at least enter into cross-licensing arrangement—all of which results in indeterminate costs.

There is also the cost associated with licensing the underlying IP derivatives, for which a higher price is expected.

When I've pointed out these costs and liabilities to many a lawyer and their bosses, they suddenly would become interested in exploring alternative ways to reach their principal objectives. While they may be reluctant to express them, it is helpful to tease those out. Why do they *really* want to own the IP? Usually, the answer is the obvious one: to keep their competitors at bay and maintain an advantage, almost an instinctual drive in the C-suite. In knowing the true objectives, the marshaling of counterarguments becomes easier.

One argument worth making: Once a commissioned project becomes a key component in the client's product portfolio, it will result in new outcomes (such as faster response times, lowered latency, smoother customer interactions, whatever the project objective). And those outcomes will be marketed and properly priced, along with the rest of the company's portfolio. That will be the real barrier to competition, not having partial ownership of IP.

Further to that and building the argument stronger: No real competitor will be sitting on their hands. Sooner or later they will develop or adapt similar products to attain the same outcomes—especially if valued in the marketplace. And while they are striving to catch up, the client will be looking to secure the next advantage and at a lower cost if their lawyer's IP ownership push is resisted.

This law of business survival is ultimately the strongest argument.

Pricing for exclusivity

Often a client wants exclusive rights to the IP. This can open up a lose–lose situation. Exclusivity is in effect a sale, but at a lower price, and with all the risks of ownership, such as infringement, remaining with the developer.

To deal with this, point out that exclusivity is a *de facto* sale. Therefore, the license price should be a multiple of the non-exclusive license. That injects some business reality into the conversation.

As well, talk about milder forms of exclusivity for a set period such as (a) excluding licenses to a set of named competitors of the client, (b) geographic exclusivity, and (c) selected features exclusivity.

Contracts are the load-bearing walls of a Lean Startup

Contracts are the reinforcing structure of the startup's house. It's non-optional to pay attention to them, and to allocate resources to them as required if the Lean Startup hopes to transform into a Lean Company and then enjoy a Rich Exit.

Especially at the exit.

What kind of valuation is given to a company whose IP is owned by others? Not much. It is seen as a services company for hire, basically a collection of contract employees. No matter how good those employees, they could walk out the door tomorrow. And for that reason, there is a limit to their value. Not so the IP.

While many founders view contracts and their legal contexts as complex and mind-numbing, best left to lawyers, the basics of contracts are truly not that complicated. Yes, the legal language should be left to lawyers. But the key points are inarguably the purview of management.

A standard business contract can stretch for pages, but key parts deserve full attention:

- IP ownership (already addressed above)

- Definition of damages

- Limitation of liability

- Representations and warranties

- Indemnification

- Definition of satisfactory work product

- Payment terms

- Duration of the contract

- Assignability of the contract

- Cancelation terms and clauses

- Confidentiality

- Non-solicitation

There will, of course, be other parts that matter depending on the situation. But having a nimble understanding of the nature and the implications of these key parts is essential as negotiations move along and trade-off decisions are required in order to seal the contract to both sides' satisfaction.

With contracts in order, a Lean Startup can move on to the fun part ...

4

ENGINEERING THE ORGANIZATION

Growing up I heard many Hodja stories, and I have sprinkled them throughout this book, as they get the points across so nicely. In fact, in my Sloan Fellow classes as well as the many staff meetings at CMD/KSC I used such stories. I am always amazed when the recipients of these stories seem to remember them across decades. The power of stories!

Hodja finds himself in need of a way to keep track of the days of the month, as people keep asking the old sage, "What day is it?" Rather than rely on his erratic memory, he develops a scientific method for keeping track.

He sets on his doorstep an urn, and each morning he tosses a pebble into it after counting the pebbles already there. All he has to do is remember that count. Soon the neighborhood kids observe this oddity and decide to trick Hodja. They sneak up and toss in a handful of pebbles.

The next morning, Hodja counts his pebbles and finds thirty-six. He adds one, making it thirty-seven. Later when the usual question comes up, he answers that it is the thirty-seventh day of the month.

Laughter results. A month cannot have so many days, he is told.

"I know that," Hodja responds. "But my scientific urn says otherwise."

Hodja may sound ridiculous here, but this is a common practice in business and scientific circles. The refrains are rather easily recognized: "But that's what the computer model says" ... "Them's the results of the experiment" ... "The study so concluded" ... "Exactly what the algorithm spit out."

There's a near-religious belief in the science of things today. Commonsense notions are discarded with little thought as to whether the neighborhood kids have been up to mischief.

This is not to denigrate scientific inquiry, of course, but instead to recognize its proper role in the engineering of an organization from Lean Startup to Lean Company—what I found myself doing as our third year approached.

It began with recruiting.

CMD still had the six MIT Sloan students working on a part-time basis. But they were now graduating, available for full-time hire. I made offers to each of them, only to be told they most likely wouldn't accept. They'd already begun interviewing around, and attractive offers were coming their way from among the hundreds of companies eager to scoop up MIT talent.

But then, one by one, all six of them (who'd graduated top of their class) chose to continue with CMD.

Why go with a startup when their options were numerous?

I don't believe it was the magic urn we kept by the door to keep track of the days! No, but I do believe it related to us trying very hard to engineer business innovation through a network of equals at CMD.

This was a notion that had first taken hold of me, like so many others, back in my academic days.

America's educational excellence shining through

I observed that some of the brightest and most aggressive students at MIT were the ones who pushed back hard on the rigorous structuring and scheduling of the workload.

Some students even suggested that they'd learn better on their own just by reading relevant books.

My response, invariably, was to urge them to drop out, save themselves, their parents, and taxpayers a huge sum, and instead spend their time in libraries developing the knowledge base that would then qualify for a degree in, say, mechanical engineering.

The point, of course, was that most of us need a structure for learning. *(Fast forward decades, we saw during the COVID-19 lockdowns how students' remote learning scores plummeted across the board.*[14]*)* Learning structures enable something both elementary and profound.

I believe in learning that is created through a network of allies— even if unspoken or unaware. A network provides students with the physical and psychic support needed to get up and attend lectures and cram for tests and slog through homework and bang their heads against the book until the answer surfaces. Surrounded by others doing it takes the sting out of it, and turns it from drudgery into, well, sometimes a joyful experience because there are allies in this great struggle into adulthood.

In my travels abroad, I've seen the educational systems of every major country. I've seen how US excellence owes a lot to its well-developed structures optimized for teaching and learning and the emphasis on validation and feedback through a robust process of quizzes, graded homework, graded classroom participation, exams, term papers, field reports, theses, etc.

No student in the United States, no matter how advanced, can escape this rigorous process.

And at all major colleges or universities, the teachers also get validated by being required to publish. These days students can also validate teachers, or at least their teaching, through evaluations published online.

It is this process of validation and feedback that I sought to build into the organizational architecture of CMD from the outset. I was inspired by the academic ecosystem and wanted to port it into the business world in a meaningful and appropriate way. To make it an everyday practice.

In that sense, I was hoping to strike a balance between the over-reliance on the scientific method and the under-reliance. I knew it was easier said than done.

So I sought to create a recruiting and hiring formula that would break with so many of the flawed practices of the time. A formula that would (a) take us into the finest schools nationwide, (b) beat out the top recruiting companies in finding talent despite being a name few had yet heard of, and (c) ensure that the talent was a good fit for the organization we were engineering.

Developing AAWE, a novel hiring mode

As an academic stepping into the business world, the classical industrial hiring model I saw everyone using struck me as stale as last week's bread. Possibly because it was designed decades before the word *knowledge* had ever been put in front of workers.

For starters, the model began with de-risking. Applicants had to bring years of prior experience or subject matter expertise. Yet in academia, I'd found that students with high aptitudes, but no prior experience, could come up to speed on a subject very quickly and then continue progressing. A complex undergraduate degree is completed in just four years with mastery of many, many subjects achieved. After two years, a student with any undergraduate background becomes a *Master* of Business Administration.

Such was rarely the case with experienced or de-risked individuals. They tended to be set in their ways and thus slower to adapt to new organizational structures. Things had to run their way, or else. After all, they were being hired for exactly that, "their way."

We wanted to go another way. We didn't want to start out with resistance to principles we were testing from academia—ideas such as *Teach & Learn, Learn & Teach ... Noisy Explorations ... Ambiguity Tolerance ... Situational Leadership ... Dynamic Configurability*—we were developing on the fly.

Since we'd seen excellent outcomes with the "green" part-timer students I'd originally hired, I sought to identify the key attributes of these exceptional people. It was not hard to assess ...

- They had a high *aptitude* and could pick up new things quickly.

- They had a great *attitude* with high energy, passion, and an eagerness to go the extra mile, do whatever was required, and work positively with a team.

- They had a *willingness* to learn and be coached.

- They had something extra, which was *experience*—this was last to be considered but still important for bringing domain expertise to the table.

And with this assessment, a hiring principle called AAWE was formed ...

Hire Using AAWE: High APTITUDE First, Then ATTITUDE Positive and Team Oriented, Then WILLINGNESS to Learn and Be Taught, Finally the Extra (EXPERIENCE)

Fair to say this principle became one of the most important of all. And we summed it up with the drab but daring acronym AAWE, often notated as Aptitude > Attitude > Willingness > Experience.

This AAWE formula for hiring would break with the hiring "best practices" of the time. It would, within a short period of time, take us into the finest schools nationwide, beat out the top recruiting companies in finding the talent we needed, and achieve extraordinarily high acceptance rates—despite being a name few had yet heard of.

And I needed to put this formula to work transitioning my own situational leadership out of most of the company functions and into the areas for which I was best suited. My functional responsibilities were then ...

- Sales and marketing

- Billing

- Bookkeeping

- Contract management

- Project and client management

- Payroll

- Procurement

- Premises management

- And more

And I was also still doing full-time teaching and research, relying on the part-time help of our grad students to meet our expanding workload.

I desperately needed to put the AAWE model to work.

The first hire was an office manager, Dave Bromberg, a freshly minted graduate of an MIT engineering program. Dave was wildly overqualified, but I went with him because his career goal was to be an entrepreneur and he resonated with *Teach & Learn, Learn & Teach* as well as *The Founder Works for the Company*. He realized he could learn the entrepreneurial ropes at CMD, and he made sure his contributions to the company were invaluable.

Our AAWE model was proving out. Mostly. To that, I made it a point to be the first to interview and assess candidates, and then take them on the rounds of the office. There was nothing unusual about that practice in itself. But it could be a sticky wicket, I quickly learned ...

I had just sourced a stellar candidate. Several national awards in systems development. All the technical chops we needed. At the same time, several of the staff had found another candidate for the position. He was light on credentials, in my view. But out of courtesy to my colleagues, I called him in and interviewed him. Even though

I found him lacking, I had him make the rounds to preserve a sense of participation.

At the same time, my stellar candidate was interviewing around the office. When I met with the key staff to review the two candidates, I was astounded that the stellar candidate was being criticized for trivial reasons—no eye contact, scratched his beard, etc. But the second candidate, who I'd found lacking, was being praised extensively. I was confused and dismayed by it all.

When I declared that I planned to go with the qualified candidate, there was palpable disappointment. Unfortunately, when I called my candidate to make an offer, he had already taken another offer because someone on our team had let slip that he wouldn't be making the cut. We did not go for the candidate that had been the choice of my colleagues (but in my view clearly unqualified), which surprised them.

I cherish excellence and talent and delight in surrounding myself with it. It was tough to learn firsthand that this mindset is not universally held. Some with excellent skills want to be viewed as standouts, so they surround themselves with the mediocre and the lackadaisical to elevate their own career trajectory. It's a form of insecurity, surely. And it corrodes the foundations of a knowledge organization—which CMD was.

> *Excellence Does Not Always Surround Itself with Excellence, But Must*

Later, I was to learn from a dean at MIT a complementary insight. When I asked how MIT manages to remain excellent, he said by getting rid of the "good" as quickly as possible. He then explained that the enemy of the excellent is the good—the good will seek and find ways to hang on, which will intimidate the excellent, who will then leave. In due time, the institution will be one of the good.

The Enemy of the Excellent Is the Good

Had I not reclaimed my function as the recruiter, the additional hires might have been just "good" and in due time pushed out even our core of excellent people.

After this eye-opener, I pivoted as gallantly as I could and decided that all future candidates would be first interviewed by me and then by a select few. In this way, the founder could act as internal recruiter shepherding exceptional candidates through their interviews with other principals in the organization.

We also discovered another reason for limiting interviews.

Invariably, someone on the team takes it upon themselves to educate the candidate about the company's internal workings and projects. But then if the candidate doesn't join on, all that deep knowledge may find its way into the hands of direct competitors. Not so good.

I've heard many startup founders admit that as their organizations grew, they wanted to continue as lead interviewer, but time constraints made it difficult. It's a valid concern. But coupled with that old yarn, "If you don't have time to do it right, when will you have time to do it over?" is "If you don't have time to find an excellent team, how will your team ever be excellent?"

The next hire had to be sales and marketing. My capacity to run this critical function was being increasingly constricted with too many other duties.

I recruited Craig Davis. He fit the AAWE model to a tee. An engineer who had interest in marketing. He quickly absorbed our company culture and began organizing our outreach activities superbly. His collateral materials were ingenious, really. I would express a thought and in no time he turned it into a graphic representation. This was in the pre-PowerPoint times, and that program had nothing on Craig.

Craig's marketing brilliance was in instinctively knowing the triggers and motivations of prospective customers. I remember our pitching so many clients as if it was yesterday …

The client would tell us, "We have our own system to do that; we don't need yours." I'd respond, "But is your system as good as your direct competitors have?" And Craig would illustrate that idea visually, showing a bicycle race underway. "All the cyclists have bicycles," Craig said, "but what part does the bicycle itself play in helping one cyclist win the race?" Craig's illustration would show the cyclists crossing the finish line, with the winner ahead by mere seconds. A gold medal being awarded. Craig asking, "Do you have the system to help you edge across the finish line in the numerous races you run in the marketplace?"

A lot of clients saw the value of having that critical edge we were selling. The message: we are not selling a system; we are selling the critical edge.

Developing much more productive teams

Getting deeply involved in hiring made my contributions to staff development more effective. It's one thing to hire exceptionally talented staff, and another to make sure they continue to evolve their talents once hired. That called for a measurement mechanism.

In the beginning I started with a simple timecard system for tracking productivity, a system we had for billing our clients to adhere to contracts that were time and materials with a not-to-exceed cap. In the old-fashioned way, the team submitted weekly timecards, I logged their hours on each project, then generated invoices along with handling the other back-office functions.

With only a few employees, it wasn't a burden. And I learned a lot.

When the staff size began ballooning, I then took a look at the time management and payroll systems on the market. Payroll was easy—there were many services. But the uniqueness of our culture made time management much trickier.

So we developed our own system using the Stratagem tool. I turned to Mike Cebry, who had joined us after graduating from Sloan after the original six had. He did a superb job in handling this.

Now it may seem like we were attacking a mosquito with a sledgehammer. But no program existed then to view time management in a multidimensional way. That is, there was no way to choose an assortment of variables of value to management—such as the employee, project, time period, project manager, billing rates, revenue per person, per project, etc.—and then correlate for performance based on those variables. But soon we had our own useful system for that and named it old-school, *The Hourglass Time Management System*.

In turn, our team's productivity notched right on up!

As an extensible system, Hourglass could grow with us. When project demands would come in from project managers, for instance, Hourglass could assign the available staff to projects on the calendar ahead.

This assignment process wasn't entirely automated, just enhanced. I would still sit down with project leads and participate in the assignment process. It was a practice that went straight to the core of knowledge development.

Left to their own resources, CMD's project managers could be counted on to assign the same sorts of projects to their teams over time. Keeping them in their lanes, as they say. Makes perfect sense. If Sam is picking apples and Sheila bananas, why switch them?

Well, if talented people are held in their lanes, that's all they'll know. If instead there's cross-disciplinary activity with Sam and Sheila switching fruit from time to time, they'll have a broader understanding of the company, be able to slot in when someone is absent, and bring a different perspective to the situation at hand. An excellent way to incorporate *Teach & Learn, Learn & Teach* into the very fabric of the company.

The benefits are many.

My deep involvement in this team assignment process offered an added benefit—being able to better manage performance reviews ...

Performance reviews become company reviews

Since I had hired our initial six employees, I was naturally the one to run their first year-end performance reviews. I tried passing on the baton for later hires but was met with fierce resistance. I didn't mind continuing with the task, since my job as an academic had been to give performance reviews to every student who came through.

I went into these performance reviews with the mindset that I worked for the company just like everyone else. Yes, I was representing the company in these reviews, but I was also advocating for the individual team member, a colleague.

The vocabulary I made up to drive these reviews was GRRITS: Goals, Responsibilities, Requests, Interests, Talents, and Skills ...

Drive Performance Reviews with GRRITS: Goals, Responsibilities, Requests, Interests, Talents, Skills

The objective of a GRRITS review was for me to learn more about the reviewee's overarching goals, talents and interests, and requests of the company. In due time, the assessment form broke down into a four-item agenda …

GRRITS PERFORMANCE REVIEW OUTLINE

1. *Looking back on the team member's performance*

   1.1. Team member provides a self-assessment
   1.2. Reviewer comments on the self-assessment
   1.3. Reviewer provides an assessment of the team member

2. *Looking back on the company's performance*

   2.1. Team member assesses the company's performance
   2.2. Reviewer comments on this assessment, and provides edifying feedback as needed
   2.3. Reviewer comments on team member's perspectives on the company

3. *Looking forward on the team member's performance*

   3.1. Team member articulates what he/she aspires to, and wants to be doing, in the coming period
   3.2. Reviewer takes deep notes on the requests of the team member for later consideration

4. *Looking forward on the company's performance*

   4.1. Team member makes requests of, and suggestions for, the company
   4.2. Reviewer outlines company plans/strategies/issues for the coming year

This assessment framework was good meat and potatoes. But I sensed that it lacked the gravy that would enable us to retain the finest talent in the land and deploy them profitably for all involved.

And that "gravy" would soon come to me. It would be based on how I graded students. Any weaknesses that I noted in an individual's work were in fact particular to that individual and should remain so.

However, any positive factors such as accomplishments, innovations, and insights should be amplified for all to see and celebrate. In this way, these positives could be duplicated by others. They could benefit the company to a far greater degree.

As for individual weaknesses, those could be addressed in a low-volume manner, so the team member felt supported and empowered to improve where needed.

Often, performance reviews result in write-ups that were filed to be referenced for the next review. For staff development to truly be woven into the fabric of a company, performance reviews need to be reviewed regularly.

What better way than by combining the reviews with the staff utilization and assignment system we'd developed through Hourglass? So every Monday I met with the person designated to do the staff assignment. We examined the various utilization plans of the project managers and synced them up when we could with the requests our employees had made in their reviews.

While this might seem like an onerous exercise with minimal rewards, it is in fact just the opposite. This weekly process made the requests expressed in the annual reviews part of the operations of the company and created shared trust.

It was a good thing I attended to this organizational structure early on, while we had some breathing space. Often the startup deals with so many life-and-death issues that building the house's foundations and then methodically adding the equivalent of rooms takes a back seat. As a result, the structure evolves erratically, like a shanty town. And later it is very difficult to tear down these "temporary" structures, so they become permanent.

Paying attention early on to organizational structure really pays off, especially when there is rapid growth. Growth is great, but if a company cannot handle it, disaster follows. Receiving orders is joyful but if the startup cannot deliver as advertised, future opportunities vanish and even current projects, poorly executed, mire the organization in troubleshooting. Not fun, and a surefire destroyer of reputation.

Fortunately, we had prepared the organization for growth by fortifying the support functions, streamlining our hiring and staff development processes, and "systematizing" our system development.

So when growth came, it led to more growth.

How could we not welcome another Citibank project?

Back when we were building CitiExpert for Citibank, I took the time to brief executives there on our groundbreaking work with USPS, noisy exploration and radiation at play. While some of it was covered by non-disclosure agreements, we were free to speak in broad terms about the value of moving financial reporting systems online.

And Citibank could see which way the digital tides were breaking. They wanted a similar system for their HR team in New York, and one for the roughly five thousand Savings and Loan banks that existed at the time—many of which were Citibank clients.

This was going to be massive. In we jumped ...

We took advantage of splitsuit teamwork to knowledge transfer the debits and credits concerns of senior management, and the bits and bytes concerns of IT.

We used rapid prototyping to build the end-user-facing parts, only then linking to the production systems. Beth Reiland, who had been a key part of CABS, took the lead on the Savings and Loan project, and Barnaby Sheridan (who was the root of having participatory reviews of almost all outgoing memos) led the HR systems. With their leadership, we delivered the promised systems on time within budget.

But then stuff happened.

Citibank's lead executive on the HR project left the bank before the system was fully stitched in. *(I have little doubt that if we had commercialized that HR system, it would be a premier system in its space.)*

That setback was brutal enough. But then as we were preparing to deliver Citibank's S&L system, the financial crisis of 1985–86 hit. S&Ls collapsed. The system we had built became obsolete almost overnight.

We had just been given an unwelcome lesson in the value of repurposing ...

Repurposing as a powerful strategy

We had invested so much time and energy in these Citibank projects, we had to do something with them. First, bang our heads against the wall. But then we thought it through. We'd carefully cataloged all of the building blocks of these decision support systems. Documentation was part of our DNA. We needed to find other companies that could use these blocks in some new way.

We needed to do in business what's done in nature. That is, the skeleton of every vertebrate is roughly the same. It's just that different parts get repurposed—for example, front limbs become fins or wings, or hands become hoofed front legs. It's uncanny how it works in nature, and in business as well if you approach this *repurposing* correctly.

Indeed, it was a keen ability to repurpose the building blocks of our systems that lifted us out of the trough of despair in which we found ourselves circa 1986. Not only lifting ourselves out but ultimately becoming responsible for the company's success.

5

BECOMING A LEAN COMPANY

As the Lean Startup gains traction and the company's opportunities are expanding, the yeasty early euphoria of a bunch of people in a tiny office all pitching in begins to wear out, and a new set of dynamics creeps in.

There emerges a sudden need for the differentiation of roles—with the stickiness of power becoming an ever-present danger. There is the need for departmentalization, which carries with it the inherent dangers of siloing and communication falling off. Some of this happens gradually but it can also come dramatically—and hurtle the company into dangerous territory.

The question is now how best to maintain and carry forward the lean culture in order to graduate to a Lean Company that remains so. For CMD, it began with ...

Opening up our first branch office

USPS contracts were multiplying in 1986 as the value-add of digital decision support systems was becoming indisputable. So, opening a Washington, DC, branch made sense. Good to be close to clients, was my thinking. An ideal location was the sparkling new L'Enfant Plaza complex just opposite the USPS headquarters.

I signed a lease and then asked for volunteers to head south to staff CMD's new office. Zero takers from the senior team. I understood. A branch office represented a risk—why be associated with that? And why willingly leave the exciting environment of Cambridge? Fortunately, a new recruit, Bruce Lynn, whom I'd recently snagged from Harvard, agreed.

What did Bruce know about setting up an office? Very little, actually. But he did a spectacular job and our Aptitude > Attitude > Willingness > Experience hiring approach passed muster yet again— and the foray outside of Cambridge grew rapidly.

On my regular visits I could see our company culture, structure, and principles taking root. This was a ringing confirmation that the company vocabulary *(Teach & Learn, Learn & Teach … Flat Communication … Dynamic Configurability … We All Work for the Company … AAWE … and all the rest)* was not only working but also enabling us to expand. This first branch experiment proved that our Lean Startup could be cloned and we could build a strongly networked company.

Students of franchises will be quick to observe that packaging the culture and practices of the original store into a rigid codebook is the foundation of every great franchise from McDonald's on down. But doing it in a startup full of knowledge workers developing cutting-edge technologies? Well, that would qualify as a different basket of fries entirely!

A Successful Transition from Lean Startup to Lean Company Requires the Culture and Vocabulary to Transition with It

We had made the first big leap. The CMD team now numbered twenty-five including our Washington office. And we'd hit three big metrics that mattered …

- We had been profitable and cash positive since Q1.

- We had solid customers with projects in the backlog.

- A pipeline of new opportunities was opening up to us.

In any honest assessment of our accomplishments, I could conclude that my academic theories and pontifications had held water. Validated. I wasn't just some intellectual from Gulliver's travels attempting to build houses from the roof downward. And yet, in the late hours, something nagged at me. I still believed and often found myself actively promoting the idea that …

An Unchecked CEO Is a Danger to the Company and Even to Society

That assertion had provoked the ire of a Sloan Fellow so many years ago. Yet wasn't that precisely what I'd become?

CMD didn't have a bank officer looking over us—because we had borrowed no money. We didn't have outside investors to pass ongoing judgments—since I was the sole shareholder. We didn't even have outside CPA oversight—since I was still doing the books.

But I did understand the value of checks and balances to protect the financial interests of the stakeholders. A company is simply a structure for people to work. An individual does not own the company but instead owns a financial interest, which can add up to 100 percent, as in my case. So to protect myself from myself, you could say, I needed a Board.

Forming a Board to guide/advance the company

Startups are wise to early on assemble a Board of experienced professionals to offer guidance and checks and balances. Someone who can be honest when many are not inclined to.

I knew of one person who, if he told me to go to hell, I'd try to find the way. I respected him that much. He was Howard Johnson—not the restaurant founder but the dean at MIT during my undergrad years and president during my PhD years and later chairman of the MIT Board. In 1986, I invited Howard to chair the CMD Board I intended to set up. He accepted on one condition: that Dr. Jerome Wiesner also agreed to join the Board.

Now that frightened me, as it should have.

Everyone in Cambridge and beyond knew Dr. Wiesner. While still a professor of electrical engineering at MIT, he led *Project Cadillac* that became known as the AWACS system—the airborne radar system that was crucial during the Cold War. He also worked at Los Alamos—when our nation's nuclear weapons capability was being perfected. Then he served as President Kennedy's science advisor, challenging NASA's choice for the Apollo Lunar Module; investigating Rachel Carson's criticisms of DDT and issuing a report in support of her claims; establishing the Arms Control and Disarmament Agency; achieving the October 1963 Partial Nuclear Test Ban Treaty; deeply criticizing the use of ABMs—anti-ballistic missile defense systems. The man was so tenacious in advancing his beliefs, President Nixon put him on his "enemies list" and cut back federal funding for MIT programming, solely out of spite.

And now I was to meet with this man per Howard's recommendation and invite him to join the CMD Board.

At the appointed time, I showed up and was made to wait. Not a good sign. But Dr. Wiesner's secretary apologized, saying he was on the phone with the Kremlin trying to secure a US visit for world-renowned atomic scientist Andrei Sakharov. I felt entirely out of place and started my escape. Just then the secretary motioned to me to go in.

Immediately I was apologizing that this little company was not worth his time. I'm sure I was burbling and barely listening, but I did catch him saying that he didn't trust his own technical knowledge in the domains CMD was operating in to be an effective Board member. Such was the modesty of this giant.

I instantly shut up.

And just as immediately internalized a lesson learned: never open with a confession. Let the other side express their thoughts and emotions first.

In our case, we were hoping to transition from a services company to a product company, and that meant giving a lot of demos of our software products. It's not uncommon for technical people, and even cheery marketing people, to start a presentation with some kind of confession. "The demo could be better but last night we had a crash" or "We are still improving this system." However accurate, opening with a confession always gets you off on the wrong foot.

*Nothing Is Gained from Confessional Preambles, and a Lot
Could Be Lost*

Despite my initial stumbling about, Dr. Wiesner did join the Board in 1986 and served until August 1994, shortly before his death. Even after suffering a stroke in 1991, he attended every Board meeting he could. Sometimes he'd show up limping, clearly in pain. But he'd always put me through the paces together with Howard, and I'd feel like a student defending a thesis when giving my quarterly progress reports.

More to the point, we now had a Board to check the CEO. In fact, at my suggestion, they set my annual salary and bonus plan until August 1994 (when the Board transitioned to a consulting Board). Even after that, I continued to work for the salary that Howard as the chairman of the consulting Board supervised until our later sale to Lucent, me without taking out any of the cash we had accumulated. *(More on this later when we talk about the founders' dilemmas: leave the earnings in or take them out.)*

Compensation experiments: gain-sharing versus profit-sharing

Since CMD had achieved profitability and positive cash flow, it was time to devise a compensation plan that would (a) keep our team happy enough to ignore any headhunters who might come poaching, and (b) fairly distribute our net proceeds.

We could afford to pay above market, and that helped a lot. But I believe our real edge came from trying "gain-sharing" instead of traditional "profit-sharing."

With gain-sharing, any cash distributions to the team would be based on first the overall performance of the company and then an individual team member's contribution.

For the first part of the equation, I developed a suite of metrics that included total revenue, customer satisfaction, on-time and on-budget delivery, and core value attainment. Some were quantifiable metrics, clearly, and some qualitative. Taken together, it was an overall report card for the company. That determined how much cash we should distribute.

Then we decided on employees' bonuses based on their performance reviews—from a satisfactory evaluation, to very good, to outstanding. This rating was only applied to the workload they had influenced or contributed to, which made obvious sense to all.

As for my own pay, I felt that our company's overall profits were determined by the actions of senior decision-makers, primarily me. So because I was evolving the company to validate my theories, and that meant decisions were made to support my mission, I alone should be responsible for and judged by profitability.

Intuitively, I felt this gain-sharing formula could work transparently for the entire team. But profit-sharing was a narrower, opaque metric involving a myriad of accounting matters such as depreciation, LIFO versus FIFO, pricing, discounts, tax, etc. In not using it, the team wouldn't have as many difficult-to-answer questions about how their bonus package had been formulated.

This twin approach of paying above market and then using gain-sharing to set bonuses definitely enhanced staff retention as well as our ongoing hiring.

*"Paying Above Market" Is Great if You Can; "Gain-Sharing"
Is Great Because You Can*

Next action item: deciding how to share company stock with a few key team members. Most startups go for stock options. I thought it would be more appropriate for CMD to give restricted stock (i.e., non-voting stock) to the key staff—particularly those who joined at the onset and continued to make major contributions.

Stock options versus restricted stock

I had our law firm, Hale and Dorr as they were called then, prepare the necessary instruments. In the process I got a big education, especially on tax issues. Restricted stock is deemed *compensation* by the IRS. Therefore, the team receiving such stock would have two options:

- Pay income tax on the imputed (i.e., currently assigned) value now

- Wait until the stock vested and pay capital gains tax then

I wanted the company to be obligated to buy the stock at full book value when it vested, which was five years in our case, but at the stockholder's option. Hale and Dorr strongly recommended a different tack: leave it up to the company to buy the stock at its discretion, but obligate the stockholder to give the company right of first refusal. That proved the correct path.

Another lesson learned. Let me explain.

This stock was meant primarily as a gift for the few standouts I had identified. So I did my best to keep the imputed value as low as possible—to minimize the income tax due. Only one of them chose to pay the income tax, even though it was nominal. It appeared the others didn't expect the company to be around in five years, so why pay anything now? Either that or it was the old "better to put off to tomorrow" way of thinking. Either way, it was surprising to me.

And I had to reflect on what that meant.

I had hired staff with exceptional potential. Compared to the mean performer in our industry, they were green but with potential. In fact, that was the point—their having potential—and I had not fully anticipated what that actually meant.

The AAWE model I'd used to hire them and give them challenging projects right away meant they were *very* attractive to our competitors. Indeed, it wasn't long before our early hires turned into rhinestone techies getting cards and letters from people they didn't even know, to crib Glen Campbell's popular song of the time. A couple of them were already qualifying to step into CEO roles at startups.

I then realized why so many companies have corporate ladders. Why they don't hand over their deep processes and trade secrets to newbies so easily. Why they spread out the knowledge transfer over time. Because those newbies become valuable targets for competing firms, and if poached, they can carry away a lot of proprietary know-how.

Right or wrong, I resolved this dilemma by doing nothing. I stuck with the AAWE hiring model. Stuck with the flat organization. Stuck with the *Teach & Learn, Learn & Teach* culture.

And I rolled the dice on staff retention.

I decided that if CMD was an attractive place to work, we could get replacement talent easily enough. And from that came a corollary lesson ...

> *Keep the Funnel of Potential Hires as Wide Open*
> *as Possible*

This is not so easily done. It can be exceedingly time-consuming to maintain a big funnel of potential hires, but it is even more time-consuming if the funnel runs empty when candidates are quickly needed.

Returning to those few now holding restricted stock in the company, it seemed there'd been a marked shift in attitudes. Since they were now "stockholders," they began to think they should be more intimately involved in the company's high-level decision-making and even receive regular briefings on the financials.

That was an unexpected step.

Their restricted stock was clearly a non-voting stock. It was offered as the equivalent of deferred compensation. But that's not how they were seeing it. They were acting like full-fledged owners. This would come to a head and only resolve itself after a huge cost to CMD—financially and emotionally, as well.

Leading to the takeaway: for a startup to remain lean, it's much better to use direct compensation, and if possible be generous by including "gain-sharing"-based bonuses, rather than using profit-sharing, stock options, or restricted stock.

USPS wanted another miracle

Having a branch office in Washington, DC, also was instrumental in growing our business with USPS, and CMD becoming even more skilled in practicing client-driven system development.

Our reputation and visibility had grown.

And as the systems we had already delivered became internalized with high satisfaction by the users, we emerged as a go-to company even among the higher-ups. Whereas other contractors for USPS worked with IT alone and consultants only worked with higher-ups, CMD was unique in working with both and, as we had done in CABS, linking both.

I attribute this unique position we attained to our AAWE staff and our practice of splitsuit interactions. Same people with striped suits comfortable conversing with the higher-ups in business terms, in nerdy clothes interacting with analysts, and in blue jeans and t-shirts discussing the deep aspects of systems and programming languages.

With such a reputation, it was not surprising that USPS again called us in but this time on a very delicate business and systems matter. The Postal Service was facing a nontrivial conflict at the Board level. One faction was advocating the purchase of multiline Optical Character Readers (OCRs), which were very expensive. Another faction was recommending single-line OCRs based on the results from a simulation model the operations team had built.

I was introduced to Fred DiLisio, who was charged with providing comparative data. Their massive internal model, which was built to include the operating parameters of almost every postal mail processing center in the nation, would take weeks to complete even one scenario analysis. And many such analyses were needed. It wouldn't do in this crisis situation.

Once again, I could see that combinatorial complexity was hobbling the Postal Service's decision-making. And I explained as much to Fred. He then asked if CMD could develop a macro model in record time and allow "many scenario" runs to compare single-line with multiline OCRs. We took on the project. USPS assigned an expert in the operations of postal centers to us. And in fast order, we provided

- Knowledge engineering

- Functional descriptions and specs

- A rapid prototype for end-users with simulated data

- Linkages to the production systems and data centers

- Complete documentation

In just a few months the system, ultimately named *META (Model for Technology Alternatives)*, was delivered. USPS was able to run hundreds of scenarios in just a week or two. The project manager was Mike Cebry, an early AAWE hire.

Simulations using META pointed to single-line OCRs as the way to go. Fred quickly realized that META could be used for many other high-level operational decisions since META had success-fully modeled the entire Postal Service operations. Now many other equipment purchases could be examined, and fresh configuration assessments of the existing equipment could be done.

Fred asked us to provide technical consulting on all META-related projects going forward. But I respectfully declined, concerned that it would warp our company and distract us from our other systems development projects. We had found our path as a company. Getting into general consulting would, I suspected, dilute our culture and distract us from our core mission. The contract went to Arthur D. Little (ADL), a Cambridge company like us that happened to have a branch office next to us in DC. ADL was big-time. They boasted a 2,500-person consulting organization and a 250-person laboratory for T&I. ADL was also a storied outfit, founded in 1886 by Arthur

D. Little, an MIT chemistry major. From 1937 to the 1950s ADL was run and operated by MIT, as Mr. Little had bequeathed it to the institute. This history would later become very relevant to my life. All I knew at the time was that ADL's contract with USPS for META-based consulting would grow to reach $100 million.

It was hard to walk away from that kind of cash.

But had I not, I then might not have run into ADL once again later in life in a quirk of fate that would change everything, as we'll see later.

At that time, with META-based services progressing under ADL's direction, Fred came to us with another proposal. He wanted us to create a settlement system for their marketing operations that would handle the settlement of payments for mail to and from the countries worldwide affiliated with the International Postal Union.

Steve Dalton led this project that produced *MAIS (Marketing Analysis and Information System)* and it became central to USPS operations. With MAIS, we were now deep into a modus operandi that had proven itself to work:

- Knowledge engineering of the front-end (the end-users) and the back-end (the system) requirements as functional descriptions;

- Rapid prototyping and iterating through splitsuit interactions with the end-users and the analysts supporting them while maintaining compatibility with the back-end (system) requirements;

- Creating the back-end links;

- Exercising the system with mock data;

- Stitching together the front and back ends so (a) end-users could operate the system with an intuitive user interface and (b) IT could efficiently manage the data links;

- Get out of the way and let the system gain internal traction on both ends so the still-small CMD would not get bogged down in the maintenance of just one system.

This worked admirably well for us. And on the final point, that is where our vision+mission confronted revenue. If we were only concerned about our revenue, then we would stick around as long as the client would have us and maximize consulting revenue. But the vision+mission approach to business argued for moving on to let the client make the deliverable their own, and not allowing them to become overly dependent on us.

Of course, being available to the client for maintenance, system refreshes, and updates is important. But that is different from becoming part of the client organization as permanent contractors. That was not the vision I had for CMD. And that is why I turned down the request to be the operator of META and many similar opportunities.

With MAIS now fully stitched in at the USPS headquarters, Fred offered it to the International Postal Union (IPU) in Bern, Switzerland. Steve Dalton and I would travel to Bern frequently to adapt MAIS to their system environment. Now MAIS would stand for Marketing and Analysis for International Settlements, in some sense foreshadowing our big foray to come into billing with ARBOR.

This would be my first experience going international with CMD. I could not have guessed how international CMD would become in years to come.

CMD arm-twisted into a name change

As CMD became established as a custom software developer, our initial haphazardly-on-a-deadline-created name now began causing us headaches.

The US Congress had decided to review all government vendors with big consulting contracts, looking for "waste, fraud, and abuse." Since the name on the letterhead read *Consultants for Management Decisions*, we fell into the "if it looks, swims, quacks like a duck" category. Government auditors figured we had to be ducks, or rather, consultants.

USPS argued on our behalf that we were not consultants. We were system developers like EDS and Anderson, who in fact had far larger contracts. Clearly we were not the ducks they thought we were. Nonetheless, someone high up at USPS insisted we change our name.

The request must have thrown me for a loop.

Because despite having taken a hands-on role in every major decision our company had made to date, I turned to an outside branding outfit to conjure up a new name for us.

They came up with dozens of choices. But all the names we liked were already taken, according to the trademark registry at USPTO, even though this was still the pre-internet era, a full eight years before Yahoo's founding, and corporate names were expected to project gravitas and bearing.

My better instincts returning, I called the CMD team together for a *blending* exercise. A *socializing* of different viewpoints to find an apparently hidden solution. "Why can't we name our company?" I asked provocatively to stir things up.

And the team dove in, offering one excellent suggestion after another—and many of these names were available. It wasn't surprising given the talent heft in the room. But none of the names felt like a

"Katy bar the door, Molly tap the keg" winner. Just when we were all losing heart, Kevin Ball spoke up. With his Harvard degree in design, he thought in visually unusual terms, and that led him to suggest … *Kenan Systems.*

Using my *first* name? I was the first and loudest to object.

But he pointed out that Kenan was a neutral name. It would satisfy the MBAs on the staff who wanted to retain the feel of a consultancy. It would also appeal to those who wanted to spotlight our software development expertise. I had to concede that point and added it to a list of names I submitted to the Board to cogitate on, absent my presence.

After only a few minutes, the Board called me back in. Kenan Systems was their choice. My protests did not impress them. They said I would get used to it. They couldn't know it'd take me years to say my first name out loud as a company name without cringing.

Interestingly, when we applied to the USPTO to trademark *Kenan*, they rejected it on the grounds that it was a last name. Last names cannot be trademarked, apparently, but first names can be. We had to set out to prove that Kenan was also a common first name by finding people in phone directories with the same name. We prevailed and Kenan Systems became official.

When our own names become part of a public conversation, we discover all sorts of below-the-surface emotions tugging at us. Or at least, they sure tugged at me. But I did come to realize the wisdom of the name choice. Young companies need a face. Customers feel much more comfortable if that face is the key person with a neck on the line. And "Kenan" put my neck on the line.

Startups Need a "Face"—A Key Person Whose Neck Is on the Line

Opening an office in the Big Apple

With all the work that CMD—that is, now Kenan Systems—had going at Citibank, it made sense to open a branch office in New York. And I loved the idea. Boston, DC, and now New York. What a great combo and each so easily accessible, resulting in me becoming a tri-city commuter.

Our chief contact at Citibank, Carlos Salvatori, was true to form as a banker, both of exceptional financial acumen and mindful of every penny. When he learned we were opening an office, he asked us to also rent an apartment so that our reimbursable expenses would decrease (the cost of our hotel stays being considerably more than the allocated portion of our stays in an apartment).

I accepted Carlos's request in the name of cost efficiency and adopted his approaches to parsimony or frugality, which obviously nicely dovetailed into the Kenan Systems notion of *doing more with less*. And our Keith Sawyer was the ideal person to open a New York office at 20 Exchange Place, along with an apartment in Greenwich Village. We were off and running with our third office.

During the CitiExpert project, we hired Bob Meyer-Lee, another huge success story of AAWE. He was recruited from Williams College and became an integral part of the CitiExpert evolution. Bob joined Keith in our New York office. (He later left the company to pursue a degree in literature, getting his PhD from Yale and then becoming a distinguished professor as well, like Keith.)

When Keith left Cambridge to run our NYC office, he was still wearing white chinos with splashed paint and splaying out across his pillows. But soon on my visits to New York, I found him sporting fine suits with suspenders, driving a Volvo, on a first-name basis with the maître d's. Was it the magic of the city, the natural transition of Keith's generation to gentrification, or both? I surmised that it was largely a generational thing, which was valuable intelligence to have in putting together future recruiting packages for Kenan Systems.

Further to that point, it's crucial to understand the shifts in attitudes and values of the generational cohort you want to recruit from. That helps in evolving a company culture that maps to generational preferences. This became fast apparent when we began hiring Baby Boomers, who viewed the world very differently from their parents. It would become so again with Millennials. And again today with Generation Z entering the workforce with its own values and expectations.

> *Employee Retention Practices Must Remain in Sync with Evolving Generational Values*

Having the New York office was a boon. The CitiExpert project became so important to Citibank that they put together a video walk-through of the system. Carlos often showed that video to visiting executives. And he had us give live demos. I welcomed these opportunities, of course, but I also knew to be careful.

I counseled our team to not forget that we were outsiders and should remain so. No matter how close we got to individuals in our client organizations, we could never get involved in the client's internal politics, or take sides, even unwittingly, or forge extracurricular links between different people or units in their organizations.

A corollary: the person you work with at the client's company is *not* the client. It is the company. It's so easy to forget this distinction and grow attached, even loyal to the people you deal with day in and day out. So I thought up a little client relations approach, gave it a name, and added it to our company lexicon ...

> *Draw the Cross and Circle It*

This meant getting to know the immediate colleagues of the key contact at the client—which is the horizontal line of the cross. Also getting to know those in the reporting chain up and down the client's organization—the vertical line. And drawing a circle around the two lines defined the appropriate reach into the client organization.

By sticking to this formula, we knew how best to network into the relevant offices of the client organization without getting entangled in the internal dynamics or politics unnecessarily.

Going west with AI and customer care systems

With our work at USPS and Citibank gaining attention, Kenan Systems was now recognized in industry. We were a fully capable Lean Company. It felt pretty good, actually, like we'd trekked halfway to the mountaintop. The median point, the old professor in me thought. But the new businessman in me thought only of now reaching out to a wider swatch of prospective customers.

Most consequently, I reached out to Bruce Bond. He had been an executive director at Bell Labs, was a Sloan Fellow, and was now vice president at US West, one of the seven Regional Bell Operating Companies (RBOCs) created after the 1986 breakup of AT&T. Bruce had a first-rate mind and we had a wonderful time digging into the projects we had undertaken at Kenan Systems and exploring where we might go next. Our meeting was a textbook noisy exploration.

At one point we dug into a problem US West and other RBOCs were facing. They were stuck with a legacy customer billing system named CRIS (for Customer Record Information System). Developed by AT&T back in the 1960s, it had a high error rate that left floors full of clerks hand-correcting billing mistakes using whiteout, no less!

Bruce had told me that upward of 5 percent of US West's revenue was tied up each month on this manual process. I would later be interviewed by the distinguished Harvard Business School professor Joe Bower about our software solutions as part of the case he was developing on Kenan Systems. I described the problem these RBOCs faced …

An executive of a large RBOC told me his billing system had an error rate of nearly 5 percent. This meant 800,000 people per month getting either no bill or a bill with errors. The industry was spending huge sums trying to solve the problem. In order to generate a phone bill, one was to keep track of every call and there are zillions of calls made over the network originating and ending in random locations. Each call has to be tracked, sorted, identified with a subscriber, and then subjected to all kinds of tariffs—time of day rate, day of week rate, quantity discounts, adjustments, and so on. And the calls can involve multiple service providers and finally taxes. And then, out of the zillions of calls made, an irate customer will call you and say, "What is the meaning of this charge—I, Kenan Sahin, did not make that call." Within ten seconds you must be able to provide that customer with an answer.[15]

In talking about this, both Bruce and I almost at once, seren-dipitously, had the same thought: Could the CitiExpert platform that we'd built for Citibank to repair their funds transfer messages also repair bills-in-error?

Bruce thought it was worth investigating. He also wondered if adaptations of decision support systems we'd developed could improve US West's operations.

We drew up a modest contract to explore the opportunities. Keith Sawyer took the lead on the project since he was a superb knowledge engineer and the key person behind CitiExpert. With just a couple of visits to US West's HQ in Denver, Keith had a handle on their customer billing problem, and we began architecting a solution.

We named it ARBOR—Automated Repair of Bills and Service Orders. Catchy, and realistically so, since it had catchy features beginning with a strategist—that is, an online decision support capa-bility that would transform the back office.

On the day we unveiled ARBOR in Cambridge, US West sent four clerks from their bill correction center to validate its capabili-ties. Fair to say, they loved it ... even though they couldn't wrap their minds around this "glorified calculator," as one called it. (Many then thought, and still think, that AI-based systems are just programs written by humans and thus predictable. Having been in the thick of it since the 1960s, my viewpoint was that sophisticated programs, especially AI, develop a mind of their own. With generative AI that now has burst on the scene, this is becoming much more apparent, and jarringly so.)

Based on this feedback, we went ahead and built a front-end interface and planned next to put all the backlinks in place.

I contacted the CIO and told him we were ready!

He told me he was shutting down the project because it didn't run on an IBM platform. *(It was a common refrain back then, for better and worse. We had migrated our development onto a Digital Corp platform that was vastly superior for our purposes, but sometimes better gets beat. And in fact, Digital Corp would not survive into the new millennium.)*

When the validators heard the project had been deep-sixed, they were enraged. They'd seen it work. They wanted it, period.

Guess who won that argument?

So to win the approval of the CIO, we ported the system over to an experimental IBM mainframe that was capable of running LISP programs. And though the integration at US West was tedious at first, ARBOR eventually took over US West's bill repair function, allowing revenue collection that was now closer to 100 percent of the billings.

Even as US West's CIO was trying to kill ARBOR, he had green-lighted a marketing decision support system. Soon we had produced *MUSE*—for *Marketing User System Environment*. Kurt Silverman took the lead, a superb system architect. He did an excellent job and we had ARBOR and MUSE running at US West.

Back in the CitiExpert and Citibank days, I had purchased on behalf of Citibank LISP machines from a Cambridge company run by Frank Spitznogle. He and I had forged a great relationship back then. To my surprise, he emerged as an executive at US West and we reconnected.

Having heard about the success of ARBOR as a bill repair system, he wondered if we could develop it into a full billing and customer care system for a well-defined area of their operations.

Of course my answer was a big yes. Enthusiasm knows no bounds.

We were put through the ringer of contracting, and I ultimately emerged with a $500K contract. And of course, I insisted that we own all the IP, to which they agreed.

Since Keith Sawyer was leaving us to pursue his PhD, I handed things over to Kurt Silverman to manage.

Now ARBOR was morphed into a fully functional Billing and Customer Care system, rewritten in Unix and C++ and with add-on decision support functionality, bringing together our two domains: Expert/AI Systems with Natural Language Processing and Big Data systems.

With each new version, ARBOR would handle a wider swath of billing and customer care functions. And right from the start its multi-server architecture could process four million call detail records per hour, while invoice preparation was measured at one hundred thousand per hour. Throughput results like these represented by far the fastest level of performance for any similar system, and faster an order of magnitude over the old systems coded decades prior.

ARBOR truly signified a new business paradigm—making business work much faster and easier and, importantly, much more accurately along the entire customer life cycle.

And in building it, we could see it becoming a powerful engine for monetizing any product or process in any-sized business, not only in telecom but beyond in media, financial services, transportation, and more.

By this point, a Denver office was making a lot of sense. Darren Walsh was willing to move there. He had been a champion of Kenan Systems culture and he rapidly grew the office and turned it into a training/initiation program for new employees called CITC for *Consultants Integrated Training Course.*

As we added more offices, this CITC program brought new employees in from sites around the world for a month-long intensive on the Kenan company culture, principles and organizational design, and the product lines. The emphasis was not on lectures and taking notes, but on getting to know the other members of the team and learning about each other's skills and experiences, naturally creating a very personal network within a business context and providing deep training in *Teach & Learn, Learn & Teach.*

The whole idea of AAWE was that these new recruits, even the ones fresh out of school, wouldn't need an extended training period, but their ability to work together toward shared goals was essential.

And by all measures, Darren succeeded fabulously at that.

He would ultimately lead in taking this Kenan culture codification into twelve offices in six countries.

Working with AT&T now meant working overseas

The word of our success with ARBOR at US West had spread to the other telecom operating companies, including AT&T. Since we had migrated to the more popular Unix operating system and to the C++ programming language as well, we could play in any pool and in the deep end as well.

And that's when AT&T reached out. They requested a confidential meeting with me and wanted to know if we could build a full billing and customer care system for a telco in another country, which they could not name.

Again, of course, I said yes. Will I ever learn? I still have not.

We went on to win the contract, once again underbidding our competitors and with a far superior offer. In analyzing why we were consistently winning bids over the likes of IBM and EDS, I discovered the simplest of facts. We were running a lean shop, with far lower overhead than our competitors, and that gave us a number of advantages.

Price, for one. We could come in lower.

And customer satisfaction derived from customer success, for another. Here's what I figured out …

- *If* a system is developed in a spartan environment with tight budgets;

- *If* it delivers the desired functionality as promised;

- It will run much better in the client environment *if* that environment is more powerful than the development environment.

This was another critical learning. Often a development environment is more extensive than the client's—generally for efficacy and speed of development. And developers will naturally architect the system for the environment they have. This relates to Northcote Parkinson's 1955 observation that work expands to fill the time available for its completion. In this case and application, systems development would expand to the capacity allowed.

Having understood Parkinson's Law as it related to a developmental setting, I sought to restrict our capabilities at Kenan Systems judiciously. Put differently: spartan good, stingy bad.

When a developer would complain that his workstation computer had only a megabyte of memory and he needed more, I would tell some old Henny Youngman joke about having had plastic surgery last week—I cut up all the credit cards. That and I was the wrong person to sympathize, since many of the fundamental computing languages had been developed on mainframes with only eight kilobytes of core memory. So if they could do it ...

Of course, my parallel motivation was to prevent capacity creep, which would lead to feature creep, which would lead to systems that ran well in the shop but crawled at the client site.

> *Do More with Less in Development So It Runs Lightning Fast in the Client's Environment*

With our work for AT&T progressing, their program manager cornered me one day with the now broken-record demands concerning IP. They were paying, so it belonged to them! So I called a high-level meeting in Cambridge with a top AT&T executive, and brought in our biggest gun, Board chairman Howard Johnson.

It was an uncomfortable meeting.

I made my case. The executive appeared to be sympathetic, but she had to depart early. Howard also had to depart, and we both thought the matter resolved as I remained behind with the rest of the AT&T contingent.

Splashed coffee changed our destiny

Turned out, the matter was far from resolved. AT&T's program manager dug in—giving no ground. Anger flaring from his eyes as he shouted words to the effect of, "No way in hell I will allow you to keep the IP."

He was also a chain smoker and a heavy coffee drinker. He had two paper cups of coffee in front of him, and clearly thought one was empty when it was not. As he continued yelling at me, he plunked one cup of coffee into the "empty" one and coffee splashed all over him.

We all busted up at that. After a beat, he did too. It took that to relax him, and he conceded, "Damn it, Kenan—OK, you keep the IP and if there are any questions, I'll blame my boss. Let them go after her!"

All along, we were fully within our rights to retain the IP. We had developed the underlying platform—beginning with CitiExpert—and had held on to the IP all along. So how, for a mere $500,000 retainer given all the work involved, could AT&T think they could claim it?

Unfortunately, many small companies don't have the will or wherewithal to push back. They fall for the claim "he who pays, owns."

What if renters thought the same way and claimed the house they are renting. Or hotel guests. Or, or, or …

Had I not held my ground, our Rich Exit would not have happened.

Let me pause here to highlight a principle I have been practicing all along.

Repeat without Seemingly Repeating

Why repeat? In my early teaching days, to make sure I had gotten the points across, I would stop a few students after the lecture ended and ask what their takeaways were. Their answers would be so vastly different from what I had said that I would be shocked. In some cases what they claimed they had heard would have nothing to do with what I had lectured about. The heterogeneous background of the students could be one explanation. But more often than not, people do not listen—or they hear but do not process or they look but do not see. Hence my developing the art of repeat without seemingly repeating.

How? There are many ways. One is telling the same story with *variations*. Another way is *spiraling*. Another is *spacing*. Once I got into this frame of mind, I realized these approaches (and many other forms of repeating) were everywhere.

For instance, in classical music a simple tune is presented, then a variation and then another variation. Bach's compositions do a masterful job. The listener enjoys the *repeat seemingly not repeated*. Spacing is also common in music—particularly in folk songs—where there is the body, then the chorus, another body, the repeat of chorus, and so on.

Spiraling, which can also be described as layering, is nearly universal in publishing, newspapers, magazines, and almost all scientific articles. First, there is the title or headline, then a summary or abstract, then the elaborations, and then the summary. They all repeat but with more information at each arm of the spiral.

In my industry experience, I found *repeat but seemingly not* an even more powerful and useful adjunct to *noisy explorations* with a *portfolio of offers*. Indeed, first time around, the prospect might nod his/her head, but did he/she really get it? Most likely not. State the point differently. Keep *spiraling* or present *variations* but always be careful not to lose interest or of being accused of being repetitious.

Now, back to the *convergence* and to the body of the narrative.

Big-company power plays never cease

While on the AT&T project, I happened to stop by a mid-level manager's office. Even before I sat down, he turned bitter. Why hadn't our Kenan Systems team been properly solicitous to him, he wanted to know. The irony of his lament appeared lost on him. Then he pressed his thumb on the table and said, "Do you realize that we can squish your company like a bug?" He rotated his thumb to show how.

I vowed to look into the matter. I also asked for directions to the office of the next person on my list. Evidently it was an "O" level person—that is, an officer. He angrily wondered why I was asking for such a direction.

"He's my next appointment," I said, and a growl turned into a frozen smile. He literally showed me the way, surely hoping I wouldn't "tell on him" to his boss's boss's boss. I didn't.

But these can be tense moments. So many people working in big companies take that to mean they can push around small companies. And they really can cause a lot of harm and anguish. Handling them with firm tact and grace is a key skill to develop.

The *cross-and-circle* principle comes into play here.

If we had not used the cross-and-circle at AT&T, and instead only worked with the project manager, which is typical …

And if I had not been able to enlist the executive's support in holding our ground on the IP rights …

Then Kenan Systems might not have become the world's premier vendor of billing systems. If I had caved in to revenue temptations, we would have continued as a custom developer of software—more of a services company rather than the product company we became.

And of course, the mother of all lucky breaks was some splashed coffee.

These kinds of battles that erupt between small and large companies are sadly common. Going into them requires both advanced preparation and quick wits in the moment. Or else a lot is lost.

Through cleverness and resourcefulness, the small company can reject the false notion that "he who pays, owns." (Am I being repetitious?)

Similarly, small companies should reject the equally false notion that the path to success lies in complete *customer satisfaction*.

This strikes some as odd.

We've all heard the lines "the customer is always right" and the companion adage "delight the customer." But just because everyone says these, it doesn't make them sage advice. Success lies in success. No matter how delighted the client, if the system fails or falls short of expectations, the once delighted client will suddenly turn unpleasant and even brutally attack and condemn you. So customer satisfaction is not the same metric as customer success.

I operationalized this important distinction in our first principles …

> *The Primary Objective Is Customer Success since Customer Satisfaction Arises from Success*

Imagine a primary care physician who runs her practice by the "patient satisfaction" metric. One patient is delighted as a pig in swill to eat unhealthy food to the bursting point. "No problem," says the physician. If the patient gets heart disease, that can be treated. In due time the patient is dying and loudly accusing the physician of tolerating the path to death. "No, no, no," the doctor says. "I kept you satisfied in your life."

Or imagine a teacher who assigns homework only to discover students don't enjoy doing it. Who knew?! "No problem," says the teacher. He can simply incorporate into his lectures both the questions and the answers. Since every gift becomes an entitlement, soon the students are claiming that the rigors of exams are traumatizing, driving them to nervous breakdowns. "No problem," says the teacher. No more exams. Textbooks are too expensive. Or these days it's the online log-ins that are too hard to figure out. So the good teacher throws up his hands and assigns every student an A or B. Students are delighted with this, but in their course evaluations, what do they write? That this course was a total waste of time, a gut course.

You could say that a doctor's and teacher's jobs are different from a business owner's—but it is a distinction without a difference. Customer success leads to customer happiness, and not the other way around. Are there exceptions? Of course there are. But even those exceptions have generally proved the rule, in my experience.

Our culture at Kenan Systems was designed to keep the customer success quotient high. We pushed back on customer demands when we believed it could compromise success. Then we'd be rewarded upon successful completion with a customer who may have been difficult, whining, and dissatisfied along the way ... but ultimately absolutely delighted.

We did complete the system for AT&T successfully, and while not every executive there was pleased along the way (maybe ready to squish us like a bug), in the end our success made them a delighted client. And for us it was a double success, as we now owned the full IP and had created the full functionality of CRIS in the highly powerful C++ and Unix environment using AI tools like Expert Systems and Natural Language Processing (now so popular) combined with Big Data-based decision support systems using multidimensional languages.

We had truly crossed the chasm, the valley of death that brings down so many startups. Many would think we were on our way. But there was another big danger that awaited us on the other side of the valley of death—lush green valleys overflowing with bounty. But alas, the natives of those valleys were very big companies that did not appreciate newcomers and were prone to fiercely attack. I call that *death in green valleys*.

> ### Beware of the Death in Green Valleys

As Kenan Systems was evolving rapidly but still a small company dealing with the giants, we got repeatedly attacked as we tried to take up residence in the green valleys of success.

Become a product company or bust

By 1989 we had grown to 150 people in three locations and I stepped fully into a sales role—because I had to. We needed more big software contracts to support our burn rate. In interviewing top candidates, I began hearing something new in their voices: hesitation. They'd heard rumors, not true they hoped, that Kenan Systems was "having some issues."

We knew the problem.

The world was fast changing.

You could see it in the business journal articles, with "custom software" and "dinosaurs" showing up in the same sentences. If we were to succeed, we needed to turn our software systems into products we could sell repeatedly across the globe.

Very difficult, as evidenced by other companies stuck in our position and trying to transition to products. A survey in *MIT Sloan Management Review* found that 87 percent of the product ventures undertaken by software service companies in the recent period had failed.[16]

Not good odds.

We had, to date, managed to clone our original culture and vocabulary but only across three branch offices. While that qualified us as a Lean Company, to become a true ongoing concern we were going to need to add products to our portfolio of offers and have more branches.

How were we going to succeed when the likes of McKinsey and Bain had failed. (Bain was a spinoff from Boston Consulting Group aiming to convert strategy consulting service into a software product offer. However, it ended up becoming another consulting firm but an excellent one at that. Interestingly, Bruce Henderson—the founder of Boston Consulting—came from ADL.)

6

TURNING A SERVICE INTO A PRODUCT

Walt Whitman and Henry David Thoreau, two of early America's great poets, both spent a lot of time in the Boston area that I would come to love, as well. They wrote of the powerful force of running water relentlessly carving its way through surfaces, reshaping the very landscape over time. Monuments of old, gradually consumed. Paths once familiar, erased. Farms and cities laid to waste. Livelihoods forever altered by this transformation of nature leaving nothing untouched. But even Whitman and Thoreau couldn't have appreciated the sheer volume of water carving up the old analog world in the 1990s.

A practical deluge began with the first Web browser and its ability to hyperlink documents, turning the World Wide Web into something useful after all. Hard on its wake was Linus Torvalds' free Linux that allowed almost anyone who instinctively knew the square root of zero to hop onto a computer and code up some new system or application. Then followed SMS text messaging. And Sony's first PlayStation. And Windows 95 that integrated the Explorer browser.

Then the Palm Pilot. Netflix. Google's founding. And with the arrival of Wi-Fi, we could now work almost anywhere.

And this is just what the average consumer could see.

Behind all this disruption swirled equally transformative waters, tearing down the old industrial base in America and replacing it with new systems architectures. "Out with the bricks, in with the bytes" was the clarion call. And Kenan Systems had developed a number of these new systems architectures. We had only to transform them from custom projects into products we could market widely in this new "operating system of the 1990s."

Nothing could be more easily said than done.

We had our own river of Class 5 rapids to navigate.

And we had to do it with the raft leaking. So I sought the Board's guidance. I thought the solution would be to divide the company in half. One side of the house sticking with custom software, the other side turning our software into products, with me managing the tension between the two organizations and not letting either side dominate. The Board was supportive, and I began rearchitecting the company.

In no time, we ran into trouble.

One group began developing the product line, sucking up resources and cash. The other group remained in custom software working for our existing customers and soon making it loudly known that (a) they were bringing in the revenue and (b) they were the reason we could even develop products and so (c) the product people should be available to them to keep up with the deadlines for our pipeline of custom work.

With this kind of infighting growing by the day, we were worse off than we'd been as a custom software company in trouble.

Back to the Board I went.

Move the product people to a different floor, they advised. I did. Create a new division, and not just the appearance of one, they next advised. I created *Kenan Technologies* and hired a new head from the outside.

Still the offices were a live wire.

In fact, the new head of Kenan Technologies was driven to tears and resigned. The senior managers on the custom software side, some who'd been with the company for years, were leveraging their clout to steal away product staff when in a pinch.

I next turned to Steve Dalton, one of our original six, to jump over and head the product group. That worked to an extent. The strong influence that he's had on the custom software side of the house was a huge help in keeping the two groups in a semblance of harmony.

And we crept forward. Still, from time to time I'd overhear water cooler talk that basically amounted to, "I brought in the revenue and should decide how it's used!"

Who in the company really earns the revenue?

Years earlier, a new hire fresh out of college had been rather confrontational in my first performance review of him.

He had looked at the rate the company was charging for his work, multiplied it by the billable hours he had logged, and computed the revenue that he believed *he* had earned. Of course, that revenue figure was a multiple of his base salary. And that multiple, to his way of thinking, was what he'd personally produced. His question to me: "How is the company choosing to spend that big margin I earned?"

Instead of getting annoyed, I sat him down for a *Teach & Learn, Learn & Teach*.

I explained how revenue is earned through the combined deployment of all the company's resources, some explicitly linked to revenue, some not, but all contributing. In this way, the consulting group does not earn the revenue that then supports the product side. Similarly, the salespeople are not the ones making spending decisions, such as the setting of salaries.

If the entire team doesn't fully understand this corporate dynamic, it can lead to levels of internal tension that doom the company. And so a first principle …

> *Revenue Is by the Company, of the Company, for the Company*

The imperative of balance

It is almost a truism that even as a company is succeeding and not struggling, some people in it struggle to maintain balance. Was I one?

By now, my own schedule at Kenan Systems had become a slog from dawn to midnight. Plus I was constantly on the road. And though I always tried to make it home, no matter how late, that didn't lighten the load.

I remember one day in 1990. I had just landed a big add-on to a master contract and was roaming the client's halls at the end of the day. As I finally headed out and wished the remaining few a *great weekend*, I couldn't understand why there were puzzled expressions on their faces. Only at the airport did I realize it was Wednesday, not Friday. What must the client staff have thought of me wishing them a good weekend on a Wednesday?

The days had become a blur.

Upon arriving home that night very late, my wife read me the riot act. For an entire year I'd only had dinner with the family a handful of times. I'd missed most of the big moments in my kids' lives. I knew it, but I insisted that I was jumping over fences and lakes to get home as early as possible. I had the airline receipts and company logbooks to prove it. "Yes," she agreed, "you do. But you come home so late the kids stay up too late themselves, just to have some snacks with you."

The next day I made a series of resolutions.

I would not stay in the office past 8 p.m. I would take most weekends off. The only way I could achieve these resolutions would be to ask others to do the same. My wife had shown me finally how all the families associated with Kenan Systems had suffered. *So I resolved that future travel itineraries would be traveler's choice, not management's fiat.*

It took a while for the new guidelines to stick, but they did.

I declared myself *Chief Balance Enforcer* or *the CBO*. At company gatherings with spouses, I let them know that if these balance rules were not being followed they should call me directly. I'd like to think they took it to heart. I also emphasized that when the company needed an umph, the staff should be willing to give that extra, allowing for a *dynamic balance* in our work lives and personal lives.

By elevating this dynamic balancing to a policy level and making it part of our culture, it ended up improving our overall performance and may well have proved critical to our ultimate success.

In software companies, it was/is not uncommon for the staff to work 24/7. But that means when a crisis erupts, there is no slack capacity. That crisis will need to be wedged into an already full schedule, and the result is invariably a lot of bad code getting written, a lot of buggy products going out the door. Which of course leads to the next crisis, and to the next, in an unending spiral.

By contrast, at the *new and improved, dynamically balanced* Kenan Systems, the team's schedule was formulated to allow for extra time in the evening or over the weekend when crises did erupt—without negatively impacting the ongoing workflow.

As for the attenuated travel itineraries, well, not many of our clients liked *that* idea. On one occasion, a major client demanded that one of our talents in the Denver office hop the first plane to London. When I called him about this, he said he and his wife had made plans for a barbecue party and he'd rather not go.

The client was quite annoyed, but I did not budge.

And in reviewing the books at year's end, I saw that our billings with that client had not suffered at all. In fact, the talent in Denver had contributed more by staying local, which led to greater success of the project and ultimately to greater satisfaction in London.

This dynamic balancing approach truly contributed to project success—the ultimate fountain of client satisfaction.

> *Dynamically Balancing the Team's Work and Life Can Drive Company Success*

> *Allowing Travel to Be Voluntary Can Also Drive Company Success*

First accidental purchase of a company

Externalities beyond the company's purview can have profound, sudden, and jarring effects. That had been the case with USPS and Citibank throwing Kenan Systems for a loop.

And it happened again.

For much of our decision support work, we had used Stratagem. The vendor for Stratagem was a small company in Boston, an MIT spinout. I opened the newspaper one day to learn that Computer Associates had just acquired Stratagem. It appeared we'd now have to deal with a giant of a company.

At the same time, it turned out, the Stratagem vendor had previously sold a version of the code to Mars Corp—yes, to the candy people. They'd been using that code in the UK under the brilliant trade name *Acumen*.

Mars Corp had actually created a separate business unit and went out and acquired some big-name companies in the UK as clients. They also placed some of the Acumen staff in MacLean, Virginia, close to Mars Corp HQ. The idea was to expand their operations to the United States, and that brought them to my door.

They asked what I thought of developing a deep relationship with Acumen. You can surely guess that I thought quite highly of the idea. And before long we were meeting in Maidenhead, a leafy suburb of London, where most of the UK Acumen staff were located.

The meeting quickly went sideways.

My understanding of a "deep relationship" was to gain access to their version of Stratagem. Their understanding was for Kenan Systems to buy Acumen and hire on the entire staff of thirty-five.

I apologized to the group six ways to Sunday, telling them we had no interest in an acquisition and could scarcely afford it anyway. They insisted that I make an offer, nonetheless.

So I thought about it, looking at the company bank balance, and came up with an amount we could afford without compromising our operations. I knew it was low and well below their market value. But that was all we could afford and with all the appropriate apologies and explanations, I put the number on the table.

Unsurprisingly, a roomful of jaws hit the floor.

It turned out, though, that one of the people in the room was a senior VP of Mars who happened to be visiting from the United States and said he'd take it up with the Mars brothers in MacLean. *(Mars remains privately owned today, with revenues topping $45 billion.)*

A month later, that VP rang me up.

It seemed the Mars brothers were keen on unloading the unit. Money was less of an issue than taking good care of the operation and continuing to service their customers at the highest standard. They believed Kenan Systems could fill that bill. They would accept my low-lowball offer, with three caveats, each bigger than the last.

We had to close the deal in two months, take over all their accounts in one month after closing, and make offers to their team of thirty-five.

It seemed like yet another impossible task, given our workload and especially with my new dynamic work/life balance edict in place. But Board chairman Howard Johnson thought we could swing it. And I sent word to MacLean that we had a deal.

In so doing, I made a hash of my dynamic balance principle. To do this deal under the deadline, I had to book meetings with both the US staff and the UK staff of Acumen in the same week. It required three round trips that week between London and Boston.

Every rule exists for the exception, right?!

AAWE clashing with traditional hiring models

In Maidenhead, I rented a suite with a fireplace and invited the Acumen staff in for a series of forty-five-minute interviews. I was aiming for the welcoming fireside chat feel. And I ended up extending offers to almost the entire staff. Simultaneously, Mars HQ in MacLean was offering each of them a one-year severance package—should they not want to accept the Kenan Systems offer.

Wow!

Not one of the thirty-five accepted my offer.

I was gobsmacked, as the English like to say. I contacted several of the standout Acumen staffers I had really liked, and asked what the problem was.

The custom on their side of the pond, they told me, was for interviews to take several days and include many managers, personality tests, intelligence tests, deep probes into the experience of the candidate, and much more. And here I was doing my interviews as fireside chats. It didn't feel *real* to them. They did like my pitch for Kenan Systems. But they suspected that the interviews, and hence the offers, were mere check-the-box exercises and that after hiring them, we'd let them go in six months or so.

It didn't seem to matter to them that our hurry-up-and-hire program was based on the tight deadline Mars HQ had slapped us with.

Now what to do?

I had committed Kenan Systems to take over Acumen and had to give it our all. So first, I rented quarters in Maidenhead and opened a one-person branch office. Then I turned to Brian McGill, another AAWE hire straight out of Harvard who had joined our product side, Kenan Technologies. He agreed to go to the UK with a development team to (a) dig deeply into the Acumen source code, (b) do the Kenan

Systems knowledge engineering on it, then (c) return to Cambridge so we could manage it there with our much bigger team.

By a stroke of luck we were also able to engage a consultant who had previously worked at Stratagem and was actually the individual who had bifurcated Stratagem's source code for Acumen.

In addition to taking over the source code, there was the delicate act of managing the UK clients of Acumen. Brian and I visited each of the clients and they seemed confident we'd be a good home for them—especially as we described the megasystems we'd built and were managing for the likes of Citibank, USPS, and US West.

To facilitate all this, I rented a small office in Maidenhead. Brian and the team worked out of that small office much like the original team had done in the cramped office at 238 Main Street in Cambridge.

Do more with less—in this case, less space, less staff, and far less time than normal.

When the team returned to Cambridge, Brian became the very successful head of our newly minted Acumen product unit. Another stellar hire, Lou LaRocca, who met every "letter" in our hiring formula exceptionally well and who hailed from Brian's alma mater, joined him. Whereas later Brian went into academia much like Keith Sawyer and Bob Meyer-Lee (and many others), Lou followed the path of other alumni to start his own company, now a very successful one and still growing.

To the delight of myself, our staff, and Mars, two months later we were up and running with Acumen's customers now ours.

As for the thirty-five Acumen staff who didn't join us, they either took the severance package or were absorbed into Mars. Their not joining us proved to be a blessing in disguise. In retrospect, how could we have afforded the payroll of thirty-five people plus all the issues of having staff in the UK?

But with no staff joining from Mars, and Brian returning to Cambridge, how were we going to keep a small office in Maidenhead operational? Well, the multitalented Bruce Lynn who was managing the Washington, DC, branch volunteered for the job. It turned out that one of his passions was Shakespeare, and what better place to pursue that with his wife than in the UK?

In due time, Bruce moved the office to Portman Square in the heart of London. Later he would move on to Microsoft, and I would hire a UK national, John Rainger, to head the office that grew to two hundred strong by 1997 under his leadership and that of Jan Wiejak, another UK hire and a Cambridge man, where he'd earned a PhD in math, or maths, as they call it over there.

With the Washington, DC, branch needing a manager, Mark Trusheim, another Sloan grad, agreed to step in. Mark would become instrumental in expanding our work accomplishments with USPS.

Wrong roads can lead to the right place

Our work in pulling off this impossible integration of Acumen led us to our first international office. It may also have inadvertently hurtled us to within striking distance of becoming the product company we needed to be.

Some perspective is in order …

- We had acquired a major multidimensional language at the source code level;

- We had acquired as customers of that language many big companies in the UK that had built big applications using it;

- We had established a toehold/office in another country;

- We had gone ahead and internalized the source code and began maintaining it;

- All in about two months without any of the thirty-five Acumen staff and without hiring any additional people (except the one consultant).

It was a story for the books on lean business development.

Accidentally acquiring Acumen through this comedy of errors was a big boost to morphing our custom systems work into products but of course a lot of pressure on our finances, our staff, my time, and an unexpected complication, but a humorous one.

So we went and bought a dating service?

Turns out, another company had registered the name "Acumen" in the United States. We had to rename and chose *Acumate* since we liked the sound of that. Soon our phone lines were lighting up with people thinking we were some new high-tech dating service. *(Match.com, the first online dating service, wouldn't come out until 1995. Maybe we should have moved first/early into that space, as well! We had all the software tools plus AI!)*

Anyway, we leaped into the herculean task of maintaining the source code for Acumen/Acumate when the target we still cherished was Stratagem—its sibling. And eventually we were able to buy Stratagem from Computer Associates. With that we united the siblings under one roof. But that purchase really drained our cash. We had no buffer at all, should we hit a wall ... and we did.

We needed a lifeline

You'll recall our creating a software system called ARBOR for US West. It had started out as a bill repair system based on Expert Systems and Natural Language Processing, hence the name, but then it grew into a full-fledged billing and customer care system. It was getting written up in the trades as a potential blockbuster and even a game-changer. I wasted no time in approaching as many telcos as I could to tell the ARBOR story. One of my first calls was to British Telecom.

Bingo, a product sale!

The licensing deal with British Telecom ran to several million dollars. It held out hope of finally sheltering us from the storms we were encountering.

But it also created a new set of issues.

These issues became obvious when I tried to sign up big hitters like Price Waterhouse and Ernst & Young as channel partners. They were accustomed to representing and/or recommending full-blown billing systems running in excess of $50 million and taking multiple years to complete. They weren't so excited about adding their markup to smaller-sized product offerings.

I'd see this sentiment at the trade conferences where I was telling the ARBOR story. Often, I was dismissed simply because Kenan Systems was not some big-name (read: safe) outfit. It was built on the old adage that you couldn't go wrong with IBM. Then I'd take the stage to stir the pot. I'd often come up right after some presenter from a big-name systems integrator had predicted with great authority that one day a Unix-based billing system could handle a million-plus telecom subscribers. Then I'd be up and say that Kenan Systems with ARBOR could already do a million-plus. And do it on a modular, scalable product written in Unix and based on multiple servers so it fits you where you're at and grows with you. Just stop by our booth to see.

I was stepping on some big toes—and it didn't go unnoticed.

It appeared that Kenan Systems had finally reached a very *green valley*, a lush one. And that we could hope the proverbial journey through the valley of startup deaths was behind us, and the future bright. But that the green valley was also overflowing with natives ready to shoot quivers full of poisoned arrows at newcomers.

We took hits from big-name companies left and right and didn't have a lot of reserves to help absorb the buffeting.

We were running out of custom software orders, and product orders were not coming in fast enough to bridge the gap. Feasts we had enjoyed since the beginning turned to famine. Our cash reserves had been blown on the Acumen and Stratagem purchases. Once again, rumors circulated that the long-predicted end was at hand for Kenan Systems. The "tell" was when some of our biggest talents internally came up to apologize that they'd found jobs elsewhere.

Bottom falls out. Is it over?

The year 1994 brought a thread of hope that negotiations with IBM and Dun & Bradstreet might save us. Together they represented many millions of dollars in licenses, plus significant revenues for data migration services that our custom software division would perform.

Then in May, IBM told us ARBOR was out; their mainframe people could not accept that ARBOR would run on non-IBM mini-computers. Within days of that, our CIO contact at Dun & Bradstreet left the company and his replacement had no interest in an external solution.

For the first time in twelve years, our financial picture was truly bleak. We had been profitable every quarter since the beginning. Now we were facing a financial wall with no cash buffer.

I informed the Board in August that the ship was on the shoals. They at once recognized the importance of resigning their positions so I could deal with the situation without worrying about tarnishing their reputations, which I had told them was a huge concern for me.

With a stroke of the pen, they transitioned into an Advisory Board. That allowed them to sidestep any liability issues and still be there for the company in a meaningful mentoring capacity. But their resignation also suggested that the good ship Kenan was likely grounded for good.

In retrospect, everyone involved with Kenan Systems—the Board, the team, and I—would have fared better if I had used an Advisory Board right from the start. I still could have paid the Board members generously to gain the benefit of their best thinking; to have checks and balances in place; to determine my compensation. But in the 1980s this kind of Lean Company structure was not available.

Nowadays the LLC corporate structure is easy to set up. So it is generally preferable to put in place an Advisory Board early in the going. It allows for all the benefits while insulating Board members from potential problems and the liabilities that come with a fully functioning Board of a corporate entity.

An Advisory Board Is Preferable to a Regular Board

Lifting off the shoals

We had two top-notch products, Acumate and ARBOR—both imminently licensable. And we had five other systems near-to-ready for market. But we were clearly stuck on the shoals in sight of landfall. Stuck where so many others had also failed to transition from custom software to products. The sands all around us were littered with their dead-end stories. Even big-budget stalwart performers like McKinsey, IBM, and Bain & Co. had failed at this transition.

Would we fail as well?

In business there is a cardinal rule: never run out of cash. If you do, you go to the penalty box, and we had almost no cash.

As the old saw goes, the darkest hour of the night is just before dawn. And indeed, a huge externality was about to hurtle a solar flare our way.

By the mid-1990s it was clear that computers were changing everything, and the old communications laws that dated back to radio's heyday would no longer cut the mustard. Some far-thinking lawmakers—both Democrats and Republicans—came together to pass the 1996 Telecommunications Act. It was a far-from-perfect piece of legislation, but it went a long way toward promoting free and open competition, advancing the technology innovations coming to market, and protecting families from the dark side of a fast-networking world.

It also meant that all the new telecom companies would need advanced billing systems if they wanted to be competitive in this new marketplace.

So they went shopping.

They found out that billing systems could cost north of $50 million and take years to build and implement. And they also found a little-known company in Cambridge with a Unix-based solution that cost only $2 million and could be fully functional on-site in six months.

From 1996 onward we couldn't keep up with the orders coming in. And like that, our ship lifted off the shoals with a bead on landfall just ahead!

Fortunately, I had developed a new sales model just in time and hired the people to populate this evolving unit. Otherwise, this sudden growth would have warped and distorted Kenan Systems fundamentally.

Let me explain.

A sales and marketing model as unique as AAWE

While building up Kenan Technologies as a product unit, I had hired four salespeople but in doing so departed from the AAWE model that had served us so well across the years.

All the salespeople were experienced and seasoned. They were "kill to eat" pros, as they liked to say, eager for the hunt. Following the traditional model for sales, we worked out exclusive territories for each one.

Soon they were generating their own leads. Following up with the sales approaches that had long worked for them. Claiming ownership of the leads. Eagerly converting those leads into customers on the terms and conditions that would delight those new customers but not necessarily Kenan Systems. My high-powered sales team was in fact thrashing our core principles.

They kept pushing back on my protests about terms and conditions, telling me, "I found the lead so it's my lead to convert in a way

I find effective." I recognized this boast as a variation on "I earned the revenue, so I get to determine how it is allocated."

I felt torn, again out of my depth.

I was concerned that the classical sales model would distort our strategic product development plans. In having little visibility into or control over the lead capture process, we wouldn't know what product we were supposed to be delivering. One salesperson might throw in "a little add-on" and another throw in a "simple side product" and soon we'd become a custom software house once again with all kinds of *little thises* and *simple thats* needing to be built on the fly into our product road map.

One example of this involved the "most favored nation clause." Basically, it means the buyer is entitled to the best price forever. If down the road we did a transaction at a more favorable price or terms, that earlier buyer would be entitled to a refund of the difference.

Lots of customers like to write this clause into contracts. Larger companies often insist on it. But I found it corrosive and even unethical.

Consider its effect on future sales. Whenever the sales team went out, they'd need to keep that clause in mind in negotiating current pricing. That would tie their hands.

Or worse, if there were confidentiality provisions in previous contracts, the salesperson faced ethical conflicts. On the one hand, the most favored nation clause would need to be honored, but doing so violated the confidentiality clause.

There were workarounds for these sticklers, but why?

Another big problem with the traditional sales model, and it's a common one that many companies face, is the "sell it/produce it" disconnect.

Sales is all about generating revenue—costs and delivery times matter little. So they are prone to offering discounts on the price-eroding margins because commissions are often based on revenue, not margins.

Equally of less concern to sales is committing to a delivery schedule that the production team can't possibly meet. "Ah, the techies are smart, they can make it happen" is the faint praise.

Clearly there are embers of hostility between sales and production similar to what we saw earlier between end-users and IT, and between top management and R&D.

With sales and production, the fighting can be the fierce—because the core skillsets and mindsets of each group are so very different ...

- *Production teams* complain that sales commits them to unrealistic schedules and deliverables. They have to work into the night and through holidays to comply. They never get a thank you.

- *Salespeople* complain that they have the deal signed, sealed, and delivered but then production messes it up, can't deliver on time, can't build what the client wants.

A scenario ...

The sale is about to close. The prospect insists on meeting with the key technical staff. The salesperson reluctantly arranges a meeting. The technical person makes the presentation. The salesperson is quiet, at times squirming, but unable to interrupt as she is not familiar with the technical details. The sale happens.

In the postmortem, the technical person says ...

"I made the sale; the meeting was mine; I moved the prospect with my technical brilliance. Ms. Sales Superstar was as quiet as a mouse. Now I have to return to the grindstone while Ms. Sales Superstar gets a big fat commission check. I think I should get a bonus too, for obvious reasons."

It seems the salesperson has a different view of the same meeting ...

"I nearly lost this sale I'd been working on for a year. In this last meeting, with the sale inches from the finishing line, this [bleeping] techie comes in and points out all the vulnerabilities just to CYA. After the meeting, I spent days doing damage control. I had to show that the competing product has the same vulnerabilities but a higher price and lower performance. If it had not been for me, the deal would have died. I must find a way to keep those [bleeping] techies in the background and safely away from my customers."

The two sides don't always see it this colorfully, of course, but often it's more so. Wow!

Three Disconnects Must Be Bridged—Between Sales and Production, End-Users and IT, Management and R&D

Considering how this sales/production disconnect was embroiling Kenan Systems, I put back on my professor's cap and tried to develop a frictionless sales model. This is what I came up with ...

- Form a marketing team whose job it is to generate leads, principally through cold calls.

- If the salespeople find any leads, they turn them over to marketing.

- The marketing team has territories for hunting; the salespeople do not.

- All leads, no matter their origin, belong to the company.

- A "triage team" decides which salesperson gets which lead—regardless of who brought it in.

- In short, business objectives trump.

What do you suppose the sales team's reaction was to the professor telling them how best to sell? Never mind that that same professor had done the key sales for the company for more than a decade. Well, two of them resigned. In an afternoon I lost 50 percent of a seasoned sales force. The two who did stay, as well as those who filled the now empty slots, loved the new model because now they could focus on closing—their strong suit.

I then went about hiring the marketing team using AAWE.

It turned out that MBAs know that the path into the executive suite often runs through sales or rainmaking, but that they really don't want to do sales or be knowns as salespeople. However, they view cold calling/lead generation as perfectly acceptable, as that is seen as marketing, nobler than being a salesperson—a surprising finding on my part.

Cold calling requires a lot of social skills and research that MBAs are trained in. We were fortunate to be able to fill those positions with top-of-class MBAs from MIT, Harvard, Yale, Princeton, and similarly prestigious schools. Mark Friedman joined us, as did Steve Alore. Soon the ranks of our marketing team would swell with exceptional talent, and they would generate quality leads that bolstered the Kenan Systems offers without warping our business models and core principles.

What's more, many of the senior people at companies we were targeting would more readily welcome calls from marketing folk, especially given their MBA credentials, while shunning our sales staff.

With cold calling and lead generation in the hands of our marketing team, I was able to build a first-rate sales team that cherished closing and were happy to receive quality leads without spending their own precious time on such pursuits. Paul English, who was among the first four and chose to stay on, was one of these standouts. Later Ed Perry joined us as well as many others who flourished using our unorthodox approach to sales.

No Matter Who Generates Leads, They Belong to the Company

Only Marketing Is Given Territories to Generate Leads

Leads Are Assigned to Sales by a Triage Team That Considers Company Objectives First

With a robust lead stream and a solid marketing-to-sales structure in place, I hired Bob Kiburz, our first senior executive. He had an engineering degree from MIT, had worked on the Apollo program, gone on to Harvard Business School, then joined a minicomputer company to rise through the ranks to become a leading sales executive.

My interview with him was very intense. It started midmorning and we were still going strong into the midafternoon when he was compelled to remind me that we had not taken a lunch break and that he really liked food! The interaction was intense because I was probing every dimension of AAWE. He was first rate in Aptitude, Attitude, and Willingness and fantastic in that extra Experience. Great all around. He joined us and became a great colleague. In due time, I would turn many other functions to him, including HR.

I believe this sequence of first hiring the less senior people and then bringing on board the more senior people is the right order. Many startups are tempted to hire in the reverse order with many "C" suits populating the C-suites.

Using all the best talent

I had been clear from the outset that the owner of Kenan Systems was also an employee with a defined share of the responsibilities. It was my best attempt to suffuse the organization with a team spirit that brought out the finest in people. And so wouldn't that eye for impartiality also mean that if my children cared to apply for jobs at Kenan Systems, they should?

My oldest son, Ayral Sahin, was exceptionally talented. He had studied cello with a Boston Symphony cellist and finished Boston College in 1990. He expressed interest in joining Kenan Systems. The area where he could add value appeared to be accounting.

What to do?

Why not treat him just like any other applicant to be interviewed for the job? So I recused myself from the process. He sent his credentials to our accounting chief, who arranged for a series of interviews. He was recommended for hiring and joined us.

A standout on our accounting team was Nadia MacAuley—she had signed on after completing a liberal arts program at Mount Holyoke College and briefly working at a bank. Ayral was assigned to her supervision. While Ayral and I would often travel to work together, once at the office we would make sure we operated quite separately.

As wonderful memories go, Ayral's talents ran wide, as he'd also studied cello at the New England Conservatory. On the piano, he was breathtaking as well, and our company parties many times were enlivened by his virtuosity.

Then came my younger son Kent. When he was still a student at Roxbury Latin high school (the oldest continuously running secondary school in the United States, founded by pilgrims in 1645) he would help me straighten up the office after our big brains had departed.

Later in 1996, Kent returned fresh out of UMass Amherst business school looking for work, inspired by his brother Ayral to work at Kenan Systems. Once again, I stayed out of the hiring decision. This one would be even trickier. A second son working at the company? It seemed wise to refer him to our Washington, DC, office. He was interviewed by the salesperson Charlie Rizzo as well as the branch manager and was hired. He had to move to DC, and gladly did.

Since Kent was in sales, he would interact with many customers and visitors who had no idea he was my son since they, like most, thought Kenan was my last name. Many times I would get letters or emails addressed to Mr. Kenan. Kent quickly showed his talents and distinguished himself in sales and later in strategic marketing. Not only at Kenan Systems but later at Lucent.

After Kent left Lucent, he went on to start his own company with the principles and models outlined in this book. His talents plus all his learnings led to a very successful company, *REAL Software Systems*. More than ninety global companies including the likes of IBM, MGM, Microsoft, Getty Images, Activision, and Hasbro would adopt REAL's software to manage their royalty payments. The clients fell into seven verticals serviced by a common platform, a big feat in itself.

As I had, Kent built his company step by step, avoiding some of my missteps and enthusiastically adopting and adapting those with proven success.

Then came my youngest son, Ned Sahin, finishing Williams College in 1998 and going on to Oxford for his junior year abroad, rowing for Oxford and then back to finish college. In one of our father–son conversations, I shared with him that I had rushed my education by going straight from my undergraduate at MIT into the PhD program. A pause might have been beneficial. Perhaps he should consider pausing a year or two. He embraced the idea and proposed that he go to London.

It was advice that would deliver a dear bill to the father in seeing the family scatter to the winds.

Ned joined the UK branch in London, again on an arm's-length interview. He specialized in the technical aspects of ARBOR—perhaps the highest-pressure job in the company because ARBOR was now our marquee product and it had to remain brilliant through successive version updates, which would run into double digits.

Splitsuiting it as well, Ned took over Systems Administration of several installations. After two years, Ned returned to the United States and was admitted to the PhD program in the Brain and Cognitive Science program at MIT. Later he transferred to Harvard to complete his PhD there with world-renowned professor Steven Pinker.

After a good run of post-doc positions, he applied his neuroscientific training to develop technologies that help autistic children learn more effectively and cope with the obstacles they face. His company *Brain Power* has received global recognition for the devices and apps they've developed, even being granted a US Congressional Award. Their success has been driven by the deep talents of Ned's team and knowing how to engineer a winning organization that had firmly embedded in it many principles articulated here.

Later Ned married Nicole. Years later Nicole would start her own company, *Globalization Partners*. The company has reached the unicorn stage. Nicole has received a huge array of awards, including *Entrepreneur of the Year* awards, and was recognized as one of the top ten women CEOs in the United States by Inc. 5000, and one of the most intriguing 100 entrepreneurs of 2022 by Goldman Sachs. She recently published a book, *Global Talent Unleashed: An Executive's Guide to Conquering the World*. It's a *Wall Street Journal* bestseller and I can recommend it highly!

I mention the stories of my family and extended family with pride, of course, but also as partial validation of the Kenan Systems model.

And one thing more on that. With my three sons working at Kenan Systems, they still had to have performance reviews, like everyone else. I always recused myself from these, and never even snuck a peak at them afterward. This was difficult, as it would be for any father. But it was essential to instilling in the entire Kenan organization a sense of shared purpose with the founder also working for the company. Nothing like unchecked or blatant nepotism to destroy that. And since the name of the company was not my last name, most people did not make the connection to Ayral, Kent, and Ned. An unexpected benefit of having one's first name as the name of the company—kudos to Kevin Ball and to the Board.

You Only Achieve Excellence If Every Employee Is Hired on the Basis of Merit

Battling for the giants around the world

Kenan Systems was on a roll by 1996–97 and was thriving internationally with the UK office acting as the headquarters for Europe, Middle East, and Asia. As noted, I was able to hire John Rainger from HP and Jan Wiejak, and together they took ARBOR across Europe.

Back in the United States we had Paul English and later Bob Kiburz, who were both very capable sales executives working several deals, reeling in one big customer after another.

With explosive sales growth, we finally had that coveted hockey stick.

Hiring was furious. Ed Perry and Bill Kantor joined us—bringing their world-class closing skills to the table.

We used the AAWE model to also shift talented people out of documentation into sales and marketing. One of them was Sabina Weld, who'd been hired straight out of Wellesley and now found herself spearheading our Coral Gables office and capably handling our Latin American clients. Another was Jonaki Bose, also from Wellesley, who moved laterally from documentation into marketing and succeeded wonderfully at it. Eric Schnadig, who had joined the Washington, DC, office as another documentation specialist right out of college, also moved into a key sales position alongside our senior performers.

Another star to join the Washington, DC, office for documentation was Sharon Lowe. And in a lateral move to marketing, she proved to be superb, later assuming many other roles.

While our US accounts tended to be in the still-forming telco industry, in Europe we were able to go after massive established giants.

We landed France Telecom thanks to Pierre-Marie Boussier, an executive of FT and an exceptionally talented leader in technology and management, and a true business visionary. The French phone operator faced nontrivial issues in upgrading their system. Pierre-Marie, a small team I assembled, and I met over and over to figure out how to bring ARBOR into their organization and make it work for them. If it had not been for Pierre-Marie's appreciation of the deep competence of Kenan Systems and the power of ARBOR, France Telecom would never have turned to a small US company for such a mission-critical product.

But it proved to be the right way.

In contrast, another giant telco in Europe turned to an equally giant system developer/integrator for their billing system at about the same time. After spending close to $500 million over many years, they still didn't have a solution.

With such a prominent client as France Telecom, we opened a Paris office and installed two exceptional French professionals, Benoit Bergeret and Isabelle Delcourt, as the leads. Isabelle had just completed MIT Sloan.

We were creating a Europe-centric brain trust that perhaps matched what we had during the formative years of Kenan Systems.

And the European teams had one more thing going for them: an effective company culture had already been developed and packaged for them. My early focus on culture captured in catchy vocabulary and early efforts to create an exportable organizational architecture were paying dividends greater than I ever could have anticipated.

And so next came Spain's big phone company, Telefonica, and with it a branch office in Madrid headed by one of our AAWE hires, Doug Zone.

Telefonica's CIO not only took a strong liking to ARBOR, but he also took it upon himself to recommend ARBOR to many Latin American telcos, in turn opening up that continent.

With Latin American operations now fast spinning up, I turned to one of our original big talents, Darren Walsh, to open our doors in Sao Paulo and Buenos Aires. Darren had been the one to establish the Kenan Systems Training Academy in the Denver office. Soon we'd learn that the Kenan culture translated beautifully across our southern borders, just as it had in Europe.

That left only one big continent remaining. A lucky encounter with Raghav Sahgal, a capable young sales professional at Bell Canada, made the difference. He almost single-handedly expanded our sales into Asia. To support all those accounts, we opened our Singapore office.

We were expanding so fast I began to wonder if we could support such rapid growth. The next year would decide it.

1

SUPPORTING SUCCESS

I've often suspected that mankind's luckiest organizing principle has been our great disparity in talents. One could invent fire but not locate the wood to keep it burning. Another could plant the seed but only clog up the great gears in the grain mill. One doctor might excel at patient care with studious attention to wellness over time, but struggle in the ER where snap decisions are required. One engineer might well excel in solving complex technical problems but struggle to communicate those ideas effectively to others.

This clear strength in one area but fallibility in another may have helped move humans out of their go-it-alone caves into get-it-together communities. And later turned solo operators into team proponents. As for our still-small Kenan Systems team, we were facing this very talent disparity issue on multiple continents.

We were forging ahead, all systems go. The dynamic balance principles we'd built into our culture were doing their job—ensuring there was usually slack capacity in our branch offices to deal with the crises that inevitably came up. But I was learning that there's a mighty difference between Customer Support and Crisis Management in a global context.

It was Chevy Vithiananthan who brought this to light. He had an engineering degree and had been hired into systems maintenance and support within our usual AAWE framework. I'd been observing his skills in handling emergencies. How he had over time become the go-to person for any of our branches stuck in a crisis. He'd assemble a rapid strike force to swoop into a crisis flare-up anywhere in the world on a moment's notice. Making sure small fires did not turn into devastating ones. Chevy was so effective at this, I decided that Kenan Systems needed its own SWAT team—a special weapons and tactics team to provide 24/7 response to clients in trouble.

Chevy headed it up.

In time, we would need to form and train SWAT teams in all our branch offices. But at that moment, I was observing that like in any fire there's always a spark. As we had built up more and more organizational hierarchies through expansion, we were losing the efficient operating model based on proximity access to each other that we had always prized and that was so essential to our *Teach & Learn, Learn & Teach* approach.

Losing control of the beast

Like in every organization, information was getting heavily filtered as it moved up the chain of command at Kenan Systems. Indeed, in setting up the SWAT teams I discovered that many of those crises we faced could have been avoided if the original trigger event had been brought to my attention early on. Yet it wasn't happening because ...

- All hierarchies try to keep problems local;

- Only when problems exceed the ability of local management to deal with them does the information escalate to the next level and even then with a lot of spin;

- Local problems often appear minor at the local level because of a lack of global context.

This was a problem I should have dealt with sooner, because I knew old Hodja's take on it. There was the day the neighbor knocked on Hodja's door in desperation and wanted to borrow his donkey to rush to town. Hodja, not inclined, said the donkey was away. Just then the donkey in the barn let out a full-throated *eeyore eeyore*. The neighbor was at once upset and accused Hodja of lying. Hodja indignantly responded, "How can you believe a lowly animal over me, a man of stature and status?"

Hodja was conveying information in the way he wanted it construed, as the truth. However, the donkey was conveying source data. Straight from the donkey's mouth.

So I set to tinkering with our management style yet again.

Even if the organization is hierarchical, I figured, the key executive should view it as flat and deal with it accordingly. But how?

The unreformed professor in me wanted to test three hypotheses related to this—even though I knew they ran anathema to most every organization I had visited, read about, or taught on ...

Flatten Internal Communications So Anyone Can Access Anyone Else

Make "Smart Interruptibility" an Accepted Practice at Every Level of the Company

Have the CEO Hovering over the Company Ever Ready to Touch Down When Needed

I jumped headfirst into testing my hypotheses, doing it in three steps …

- Moved my office assistant away from my door.

- Kept my door open whenever I wasn't in a focused meeting or on a critical phone call.

- Told the entire office that anyone could walk in and interrupt me anytime the door was open, and I would in turn be doing the same.

So how did it go?

Within days, I was being given unfiltered information I previously knew nothing about. Often this information became immediately valuable. I could view it within the global context of the company—something nobody else at the company could. And I could quickly determine whether some brewing crisis was in fact a dumpster fire that'd be self-extinguishing or instead a three-alarm house fire requiring the immediate deployment of our SWAT team.

There was another unexpected benefit and discovery. One would expect that two employees with offices next to each other would know what the other was doing. As I hopped from one office to the other,

I was shocked at how siloed information was. The outcome: I was acting as a link between and among these silos. In due time, that lateral transfer of information also became part of our culture and substantially reinforced our core *Teach & Learn, Learn & Teach* principle. (Repeating with a variation!)

From that day forward, I saw my own role in the company through new eyes, or rather, altitude. For I now fancied myself a manager on a zip line hanging on with a bungee cord running over the company and ready to lower into any situation when needed, deal with it, then zip back out or away.

Later the management gurus Tom Peters and Robert Waterman would popularize management by walking around (MBWA, they called it) to keep in touch with employees and gain a better firsthand feel for the workings of the company.[17] And today, the practice is commonplace.

But back then, the concept felt novel, even a bit scary. Or at least it did until it worked. Kenan Systems' strategic emphasis on flattened communications, smart interruptibility, lateral connectivity, and CEO-on-a-wire paid off on the organizational metrics that mattered. I got to know our employees much better, so I could …

- Help our employees in their daily workflow;

- Swiftly identify problems in the making, and deal with them;

- Foster a culture of collaboration and continuous learning.

Dealing with the hidden agendas

A corollary to the filtering problem is the agenda problem.

Information filtered up from floor to floor in the company is subject to the agendas of all who touch it. And while in a perfect world, everyone in an organization would be on the same agenda, we of course know that to be far from reality.

Another Hodja story tells us how far.

One morning, Hodja is confronted by his next-door neighbor about the huge racket coming from Hodja's house. Hodja says it was his coat tumbling down the stairs. The neighbor could just accept that answer, but he's the skeptical type and presses Hodja. "OK," Hodja says, "I was actually in the coat." Now that seems more credible. But the nosy neighbor probes further and Hodja admits, "Truth be told, my wife tumbled down with me and my coat."

Hodja's agenda clearly drove his sharing of information. We recognize this often in politicians who are renowned for telling nothing but the *partial* truth. But woefully, so are many scientists. In their published papers, a great deal of detail is omitted or buried so the focus can be kept on "novel" findings that will get them noticed. *(That is why, by the way, many "scientific" findings reported in top journals and hyped in the media and hijacked by politicians with agendas cannot be duplicated in reality.)*

This has become even more important today, for as we mentioned earlier, modern companies are often seen as the face of the founder or key player. Think of Steve Jobs and now Tim Cook at Apple, Mark Zuckerberg at Facebook, Jeff Bezos at Amazon, Elon Musk at Tesla. This kind of superstar phenomenon is relatively new.

Top dogs in older companies once tended toward lower profiles. Few outside of industry in the 1970s knew that Edward N. Cole ran GM and brilliantly gave us the Camaro, or that Thomas J. Watson Jr. was CEO of IBM and transitioned the company from a maker of punch card equipment to a leader in computing.

But today we know the men and women in charge. Often, we know them too well because of the always-on media culture. The face of the organization is now the focal point for any praise or condemnation the company is believed to deserve. And yet, ironically, that "face" often cannot see the organization as clearly as the outside world can through social media.

Pre-internet, employees enjoyed only a limited reach into the outside world. It was essentially landlines and letters. Now there are a multitude of ways to fire off information, and each receiver can be a powerful multiplier by sending it on to a new network, so that within minutes that information could be on the lips of billions of people around the world. And who do those people associate with that information?

Yes, the face of the organization.

Today's businesses are effectively operating in a building where all the walls and floors are made of glass. Executives on the top floor can see across their floor, and they can see the tops of heads one floor below, but further down gets opaque. But for the outside world, every floor is visible and for them, the organization is flat in terms of visibility.

That is why it's so important to convert hierarchical organizations into ones with flat communications internally and two-way interruptibility an accepted norm. This encourages information flow, allows for validation at every step of the filtering, and puts executives in a position to not only detect fires in the making but snuff them out before having to call in the SWAT team.

Client advocates—another layer, but valuable

As Kenan Systems continued to grow, our project managers got more and more overwhelmed with their duties and deliverables and unable to dredge up the hours needed to effectively interact with the client and nurture the relationship. Or they were so focused on the urgent matters of one client, they unintentionally ignored the needs of another.

So I experimented with a new role in the company: Client Advocate. It was not a decision made easily, because this would add a layer of complexity and cost to client service. But I kept a keen eye on this new role, to gauge the value-add, if any.

These advocates had direct access to the client and to key people at Kenan Systems as well. They could see "both sides" of the relationship and be genuinely effective advocates for the client. And those clients were free to reach out to the advocate at any time, to register any concerns they had.

Before long, these advocates paid out. They became valuable two-way links offering many benefits over and above the line-item cost of bringing them on. They also improved our overall client satisfaction and enhanced the success of our products, importantly.

This new position also helped in new client acquisition. Often when I was about to close a sale, I would "throw in a Client Advocate" to enhance the offer. And it did lead to more successful closings. It tipped the margin, I believe, because enterprise executives were all too familiar with the close-and-dispose mentality of our industry (digging deep into client's interests through to the close of sale often involving senior staff, then brushing off those interests afterward and delegating to junior staff, a form of bait and switch).

"Close-and-dispose" had no place at Kenan Systems, even more so after we installed Client Advocates, I was proud to say.

Support functions—the hidden drivers of success

No company attains excellence without a top-notch support staff. And that can only happen when support is heralded as core to the company's culture and practices. At Kenan Systems, we tried to craft support functions that were truly lean, but never mean. The easy rhyme of those words masked the difficulty of executing on the principle.

In the area of HR, we held out for a long time with no formal office. But even our chief-cook-and-bottlewasher-minded CEO knew we needed one. So long after I should have, I went out and recruited Ileen Winnick to run HR.

Ileen came with an impressive track record in business—the E in the AAWE model (Experience). This was a slot for which relevant experience mattered greatly. There were so many rules and regs that began mattering more as a Lean Company. And Ileen would have the unenviable task of shoehorning compliance with these rules and regs into our increasingly unique Kenan Systems culture.

In her first interview, I told Ileen we wanted a *disempowered* HR director to run a *disempowered* HR department. I think I offended her. She was, after all, a Cornell graduate experienced at big-name companies. But she was interviewing at a small company where she'd be given little power, or so she thought. She had to be wondering why she'd even bothered to show up. But before she attempted a tactful retreat, I explained what I meant.

Most companies have *empowered* HR—especially at the enterprise level. In these companies, the managers have to submit job descriptions to HR and then wait and wait for the HR magic to happen, until voilà, a new hire shows up. Or the managers need to make a job adjustment, or a pay raise, or a hundred other HR things and that means trudging over to HR to get it done, someday. All too often, managers learn to dread HR and hatch plans to end-run that office.[18]

That's why I wanted to strengthen HR by *disempowering* it. HR would become like *consultants* to the managers, tasked with delivering on the managers' needs, helping to advance the AAWE hiring model as the company expanded. Managers would hold HR in higher regard as their internal support and HR staff compelled to act as internal consultants, not as decision-makers, and everyone would be happier.

Ileen got it and joined us. She also became a champion of our hiring models. With her and others we expanded our HR team to be highly effective even as they remained disempowered and became highly sought after. In disempowerment they had impact and hence *implicit* power.

Oh the glory and heartache of Legal

To the extent that Kenan Systems made a mark in business, it was due in large part to our handling of IP. Our way of writing contracts so that both sides won. Our crossing of every *i* and dotting of every *t* (yes, the littlest things can slip). We saw it as essential for evolving from a Lean Startup to a Lean Company.

It was, in every way, the backbone of our ultimate success.

So I remained involved in every contract negotiation until our exit and even beyond. I believe I discovered the secret to actually enjoying contracts! That was, simply enough, that only a handful of things really matter. Get clear on that handful, and the rest is just boilerplate.

But prior to my "discovery," I did rely on outside law firms. They'd draw up contracts that weighed as much as I did, or it sure felt that way. I didn't mind their billable hours—OK, not true, I minded. But I minded even more that those long, tortured contracts didn't appear to yield better results.

So as soon as the budget allowed, I hired Mike Musi as an in-house lawyer. I shelved our AAWE hiring policy for this and went with Experience, alas without fully testing for A and A and W, as I had done with our HR hire, Ileen. I was in too much of a hurry because of the deluge of contracts coming in. Alas, I had to deviate from one of my cardinal principles: be fast but never in a hurry. I hurried.

Within a few years, the legal team had grown—each addition an exceptional legal mind who also taught on the side. They were excellent in our direct negotiations, especially Carol Levasseur and Charlene Fryou.

Yes, you could say I was happy with legal. And yet ...

A habit of mine, going way back, was to keep track of my hours. A simple pencil-and-paper timesheet worked just fine back then. And in reviewing my hours, I found that +/–25 percent of those hours were spent negotiating the very same contract clauses with new prospects over and over.

And these clauses that our lawyers inserted into each contract felt confrontational, not collaborative. They were acting like an outside law firm—very legal and aiming to protect us against distant risks but hampering my ability to negotiate effectively now. Not good. Any effort to promote healthy business relations based on the shared goals of the two parties was in their view ... incidental. A big disconnect was growing bigger and I was struggling to wrap my mind around it.

For example, the most important part of the contract is the Statement of Work (SOW) and yet the lawyers buried it in the Appendix and left it mostly blank.

Hmmm.

For starters, why couldn't the contract open up with the SOW and then toss all the Terms and Conditions (T&Cs) into the Appendix? It just made sense to start with what we were promising to do and negotiate that. Then, in a non-confrontational way, hammer out the T&Cs.

Our Kenan culture had evolved from an early decision to never sue a client—unless forced to by truly egregious behavior. Fortunately, that had not happened. So what was the point of starting a contract with threatening clauses, leading to counter clauses by the other side?

My lawyers surely had a private laugh over this set of asks. Mike Musi, who at the time was heading the team, told me I didn't really understand how contracts worked. Perhaps so, but I was reluctant to give up.

Why not just do it? I banged out a four-page sample peace contract. The legal team, especially Carol Levasseur and Charlene Fryou, polished up the language and formatting, resulting in negotiations becoming so much more productive and fun for me.

This contract basically reversed the traditional structure, putting the real meat and potatoes of the workplan and pricing first. It meant I was implicitly tying agreement over the SOW (deliverables, the timing of, and prices) to the T&Cs. If the client's legal team came charging in later to propose some "little addendum" such as an unreasonable warranty, I'd offer a rehearsed line, "OK then, we must increase the price by XX% since that warranty is a form of insurance and logically the client pays for the client's extended insurance policy if the client desires one."

It was a powerful argument, as it turned out.

I had similar arguments prepared for other standard clauses. For instance, when client lawyers tried to push on us unlimited liability, and they often did, I shared that our accountants would have to reflect that in our financials, devaluing the company, and how would the client benefit from associating with a weakened partner?

Plus the very idea of unlimited liability is contrived, at best. Truly, the limit of liability is always the financial capacity of the company. When the lawyers stood firm anyway, I then insisted on fair-minded symmetry—that is, the client agreeing to unlimited liability, as well.

None wanted to, as it turned out.

We would then agree that the liability would be a reasonable multiple of the size of the contract. We would also agree on a reasonable "cure" (the period of time a party has to correct a breach of contract). It's important to pay attention to this "innocent" clause (specifies how the indemnified party will be protected by the indemnifying party in the event of a claim or loss). If the cure period is too short, then the client could later use it to cancel the contract and demand a refund, or damages.

Another typical T&C is the "acceptance clause" (the conditions under which the product will be accepted by the customer). Typically, client lawyers try to leave this one open-ended, even demanding that payment be contingent on acceptance. That's OK, but when does this acceptance happen? If left to the client, it might not happen until well after the system is in production.

Worse, they can claim that new issues keep arising and that they need fixing—at no cost. This is obviously a path to ruin. So I regularly set acceptance periods to a fixed time such as one month. Either that or when the system went into production, whichever came first.

Write "Peace Contracts" That Put the SOW Up Front and the T&Cs in the Appendix

> *Insist on Reasonable Acceptance Plans for Deliverables*

Another innocent-looking snare is "precedence." If there is a conflict in the terms of the SOW and the T&C, which takes precedence?

Sometimes a client lawyer will act all innocent and stipulate that the SOW terms take precedence, which would seem appropriate. But what if the T&Cs have been carefully negotiated in relation to the current SOW, and then there is a second SOW down the road that could include terms that override the original SOW?

The danger here is that when the project is well underway and the SOW is being written by operational managers, the client could easily insert novel terms that render the contract toothless. Lesson: make sure the key clauses of the T&Cs rule if there is a conflict with subsequently inserted terms in a downstream SOW.

Only a handful of T&Cs are consequential, and the CEO must be skilled in negotiating them. Even if that means taking a short course in business contracts, it is simply essential.

Getting the debits and credits right

As a Lean Startup, I was handling many tasks and functions, including accounting. It wasn't hard in the beginning, since there weren't a lot of debits or credits.

Accounting is similar to legal in important ways. When you consider all the regulations and the IRS's thick codebook, the picture looks beyond the comprehension of your average entrepreneurial founder. But once again, the key bits of accounting must be understood by the CEO who aims to remain in charge of a Lean Company.

Two items merit a closer look: billing rates and overhead.

At the onset, Kenan Systems contracts were time and materials, with a not-to-exceed cap. Sometimes there were milestones for payments, but generally we submitted monthly invoices.

While commercial contracts have negotiated rates, the US government time and materials contracts have provisional rates based on estimated direct labor rates, plus a markup. At the end of the year or billing period, the company submits actual costs, and the differences are reconciled. Also, the government reserves the right to come in and audit actual timecards, as well as costs. And certain costs—such as interest on loans, marketing, public relations—cannot be included in overhead, so-called excluded costs. Also, the government can restrict the markup on the total cost to about 10 percent, unless it is a fixed-fee-plus-cost contract.

We were fortunate to begin in business with USPS as a client, since it forced me to learn the billing processes and basics of government contract regulations (known as FAR, for Federal Acquisition Regulations).

Billing minutia is often a third area that founders tend to shy away from. But as with certain legal and accounting precepts, billing must be well understood or else huge opportunities and revenue, including being competitive in bidding on jobs, are sacrificed. The basic process is simple and can be learned in a few hours. The details are tedious, but not the overall schemes.

Basically, billable staff can be budgeted into labor categories. The average compensation for each bucket is then computed. The standard year is 2,080 hours (fifty-two weeks times forty hours). Vacation hours, sick time, and personal time are then subtracted to arrive at the billable year in hours. Typically, it is around 1,800 hours. So the labor category average compensation divided by the hours in the billable year gives the direct labor cost per hour (LC/hr). Then one estimates the expected utilization for each labor category, which runs about 70 percent for a busy company.

That means 30 percent of those typical 1,800 hours, or about 540 hours, are not expected to be billed. They might be for training, downtime, etc. For each employee being billed for, the estimated LC/hr times 540 hours goes into the overhead cost pool.

General overhead expenses (like rent, support staff compensation, utilities, etc.) are added to the overhead cost pool. This one big pool, divided by the total expected hours for all direct staff to be billed, is the overhead multiple.

There are different schemes for allocating overhead costs, which leads to different billing rates. But once the scheme is understood, the executive can guide accounting in setting up revenue-maximizing billing rates.

The differential in revenue between a poorly computed rate and an optimal one can be enormous. I learned all this on the slow boat.

Today, of course, there are turnkey accounting packages that can aid the founder. It is still incumbent on the founder to invest in learning how to run the software, especially for cost allocation and rate computation.

There's also the side benefit of being able to track financial performance far more knowingly, thus guiding the organization accordingly.

Case in point ...

A coffeeshop owner is approached to have soda vending machines installed at no cost in a space not otherwise being used. The owner would get 10 cents for each can vended. Looks like free money, the owner thinks.

His CPA disagrees.

The CPA uses an "allocated cost" analysis to figure out the square-foot rental cost, along with utilities and other costs, which show that each can vended would cost 20 cents, a bad deal.

A simplistic example, yes. But many startups follow that CPA's allocated cost approach and miss the opportunities that "marginal cost" analysis would bring in. In this case, that unutilized space is going to cost the same whatever. Having a vending machine there that generates 10 cents per soda is a bonus and might bring in more customers.

At Kenan Systems when I finally, reluctantly, went looking for an outside CPA, I again broke my rule as I had done with the legal hire. I departed from the AAWE model and hired a seasoned accountant, Joe Vanni, as the controller. His performance was classically rigid and not at all compatible with our culture. Suffice it to say, along with the finances of the company, I suffered. Fortunately, a few years later, I hired Jay Adams, who had just graduated in accounting from Boston College. And yes, I used our AAWE model to hire him. When Joe quit in the middle of a difficult period, Jay went on to become our comptroller and capably run both accounting and banking relations with just a few staff—even when we neared one thousand employees across numerous international branches. He transitioned into Lucent and continued to perform well there.

As a privately held company, we were not required to perform audits. But I was a champion of checks and balances, and external validation. I began having external audits back in 1986, when the Board was formed. Through them, I got a very good sense of the operations of the company.

Audits are expensive, plain and simple. Almost as effective are accounting reviews, which cost far less. The only difference, really, is the audit letter that accounting firms issue to you. And that is qualified anyway. I highly recommend accounting reviews for a Lean

Startup, and without reservation for a Lean Company. While my business strategy had never included an exit, having audited financials for fifteen years was critical when we did choose to exit.

External audits/reviews augment checks and balances, which promotes Rich Exits.

From our personalities, our passions emerge

Often when hiring, I did not find out an applicant's true talents until well into the process. As I've discussed, I would use the AAWE model as often as possible. And I would later do performance reviews using the GRRITS model. But it was only from an individual's personality that their true passions emerged.

I learned this rather starkly.

A letter I received with an attached résumé told me that Aidan Lloyd, who had finished Harvard with a BA degree, wanted to do C++ utility coding. That surprised me, but I did contact him and he was true to what he said and was hired. He did an excellent job adding to our C++ library of utilities.

Wanting to do staff development and a little worried that with Aidan's broad background, he might have been pigeonholed into a narrow function, I offered to take him on a sales and marketing trip to Washington, DC. He patiently accompanied me to my various meetings. On the flight back, he politely inquired if people really enjoyed such activities. Clearly, his personality, his interests, and his passion all converged on C++ coding and that is what he did for years.

There is another aspect to this, as embodied in the Peter Principle. When employees succeed and the reward is a promotion, sometimes that promotion takes them to a job where their personalities, interests, and passions might not converge, and they become underperformers.

Hence the Peter Principle that some people are promoted to their level of incompetence. Imagine if, without understanding this, I had moved Aidan into sales and marketing?

One of the hats I wore too long was, in fact, operations. It was well past time I delegated that. I knew it would require a person with the right temperament and personality and, of course, aptitude. Who better than Peter Schnoor, a later hire who now was in charge of operations?

In this case, Peter was promoted to his true level of competence. He was the pillar we rested on in so many office moves. He was a mastermind of assigning staff, often a treacherous task. He excelled in so many operations-related activities, people just accepted his decisions. One did not quarrel with Peter.

Lean versus bloated management

It happens more when the VCs get involved. It happens more now with Millennials thinking they need a "senior" or "C something something" in front of their name. Whatever the reason, many startups right away mint an array of C-level titles—CFO, CIO, CTO, COO, CRO, CHRO, CYA (yes, even). And out of the gate, they are top-heavy, likely to remain so. Too many leaders, too few followers, as we used to say. It is always better to start lean, forcing the founders to pick up the basics of accounting, HR, legal, operations … and then build up supporting teams.

This calls to mind the five managers who gather to discuss the terrible crisis their company is facing. After rounds of cost-cutting and layoffs, the company is still bleeding. There is now only one worker left, along with the five managers. After a long and heated discussion, they agree it is best to fire the remaining worker—to cut costs to the bone.

Sounds ridiculous, of course, and yet management always finds it easier to cut the workforce than their own ranks. Instead, managers should be held to a metric along these lines: spend 5–10 percent of total hours on management, the rest of the time participating in the workload—sometimes writing code, other times cleaning the kitchen, always learning other team members' tasks so they can be valuable when needed outside their immediate domain.

Success leading to unwanted visibility

By 1998, Kenan Systems had become the go-to company in billing and customer care, but we had yet to penetrate the utility industry. That was largely because of the arcane billing systems utilities were known for.

Then automatic meter reading came along. And we found ourselves in the position of adapting ARBOR to utility billing, as well.

Endless possibilities now awaited us.

Plus, we hadn't yet fully productized the five decision support systems still sitting on our shelf. That, and we had a full complement of channel partners in place, having enlisted the big-name giants who a decade earlier had snubbed us. Now they were happily selling our products, adding their own markup.

With the company so well established and financially secure and its culture deeply rooted, I had more courage in hiring. But I still used AAWE but now with more emphasis on the E, which meant more senior people.

On the billing platform front, our only credible competitor was Amdocs. They had an excellent system, but they had to build it from components as opposed to our well-integrated ARBOR platform. In head-to-head matches, we usually got the nod.

All in, we were growing 50 percent a year and headed to 100 percent a year judging from the lead funnel. And our margins, owing to our remaining a genuinely Lean Company, were hovering around 50 percent. Cash was accumulating fast and furious.

Through this yeasty time, I kept a low profile and kept mum publicly about the financial success we were enjoying. Only the controller and I fully knew the financials because, as mentioned, our Board had become advisory.

Likely since we hired heavily from Harvard Business School, we caught the attention of its distinguished Professor of Business Administration, Joe Bower. He asked to run a case study on Kenan Systems and our many innovative successes including *AAWE … Situational Leadership … Flat Communications … Service to Product Transition … Upscaling through Modularity … Client Advocate Managers … Splitsuit Management … Gain-sharing … Customer Success over Customer Satisfaction … Dynamically Reconfiguring the Organization … Disempowered HR … Staff Development as Weekly Assignments*, and more.[19]

Professor Bower told me he used this case study in his teaching for at least ten years, and several Harvard grads that we interviewed for jobs had the good sense to mention as much early in their interviews!

Through these good times and previously the bad, as well, I had managed to my great personal satisfaction to steer clear of Wall Street entanglements. The great validation experiment was coming along well. Our coffers were full of cash and our client set was stellar with our products in much demand. And I had the great satisfaction of working with exceptional staff. Even if I had gone on teaching at MIT or elsewhere, I could not have had such a group of talent as my students. Any link with the "money" community would quickly warp and shift the fundamental thrust to the standard dogma (with which I do not agree to this day) that the business of business is to maximize profits for the shareholders. *Maximize* and *profits* and *shareholders* are ill-defined terms. Better terms are *satisficed* and *value gain* and *stakeholders*. However, my pontifications on this soap box are best deferred to another time.

It wasn't always easy to remain incognito. My receptionist and I got duped once when the caller said Judge Collins was calling. Curious that a judge would be calling, I answered, only to be told by the intermediary at the other end that "Mr. Judge Collins will be on the line shortly, please hold." Clearly a call from an investor, and I chose not to hold.

Here is another encounter, this one rather humorous.

On a visit to Rome, I was having lunch in a restaurant at a piazza. Seated nearby was an American couple, and so naturally we got chatting. The usual. Where do you live? What do you do? They went first. The woman said she worked at a big Wall Street investment house. When asked, I told them I worked for a small company they wouldn't know. She persisted, and so I said Kenan Systems. Suddenly she got animated and swore that the CEO of Kenan Systems was "the biggest jerk" since he never returned her calls. She then asked what I did at Kenan Systems. Sheepishly, I admitted to being that rude CEO.

Having never taken Wall Street's calls, I didn't figure it would change late in the game. What I didn't know was, despite my keeping a low profile, Kenan Systems had caught the attention of major investment banks and major telecommunication companies.

8

THE RICH EXIT

We had reached the mountaintop to find a table, chairs for all the lawyers and executives, and a single goal—negotiating our Rich Exit.

Our little company, started on a shoestring $1,000 in 1982, now boasted 750 knowledge workers and projected 1999 revenues of $200 million-plus with EBITDA of $110 million. Our fair market value was at least $3 billion. But price had never been my first concern, and it wasn't now as we all sat down at the table.

Much more important had been my goal of field testing my ideas about engineering the ideal organization, which expanded over time into transforming a big corner of the software market and even impacting our acquiring partner, Lucent, with its legendary Bell Labs.

I fully recognized just how audacious I was being. And had no illusions about achieving all that I desired. How could our relatively little firm, no matter how many MIT and Harvard graduates we counted, significantly impact a 136,000-employee company with its long and storied history of inventive genius?

That was the very definition of audacious.

Yet sitting at that table, I first insisted on special conditions in the contract. The main one: our Kenan Systems technical team of about seven hundred would officially become Members of the Bell Labs Staff under the Lucent banner, giving our team that most coveted "MBLS" title. And giving us a chance to work alongside the finest minds of our time to build the future of telecom.

Being granted that wish, I was perfectly happy to sign over the Kenan Systems title for a $1.54 billion payout, a 50 percent discount from the value JP Morgan had established.

That meant Lucent was acquiring our Kenan Systems business models, principles, and practices. And hopefully for good. It also meant my team and I would be starting with our MBLS titles in Summit, New Jersey, in February 1999. I was also made a VP of Technology at Bell Labs. I did not request it but when given that responsibility, I didn't push back.

Could Jersey be my Cambridge South?

In every acquisition negotiation, a big question is raised by the acquirer, and it's raised knowing the answer they want to hear. Will the CEO of the company be staying on or making a clean break?

Most often the acquirer wants to slap golden handcuffs on the CEO, keeping that key person around for at least a couple of years to ensure a smooth transition. And those handcuffs come with performance expectations linked to compensation. That is, if we make more money from this, you make money from this.

In my case, the negotiations could not have been cleaner. In fact, in all my years of teaching Sloan students, I had never witnessed an acquisition case study that was so ... straightforward. Purchase price paid up front in stock convertible to cash in just thirty days after closing. No contingencies or warranties to figure out. Kenan Systems owned the rights to everything we sold. There were no ongoing lawsuits or other encumbrances. No debt and hence no banks involved—and only one shareholder.

So Lucent knew exactly what they were getting.

They knew our internal systems were fully mature with a product upgrade road map all laid out nicely on a good-looking Gantt chart.

They knew they could capably take over sales and marketing of ARBOR and our other products.

So they asked only that I stay on for one month past the closing date.

I chose to commit for two years. But I wanted Kenan Systems to be a wholly owned subsidiary of Lucent/Bell Labs, with me continuing to run it with full autonomy for at least one year. I would report to the group president of the Software Communications Group but would not take orders from him. Directions I would consider, but orders, no. I saw that as an essential step. It meant that our Kenan Systems team would have a warrior fighting for their successful integration into a much-larger, much more politics-driven company. I didn't know what lay ahead, but I knew how large companies tend to operate.

For me, this decision to "join" Lucent/Bell Labs for at least two years was deeply personal and multilayered, as it would be for any founder. I cannot recommend staying on, or leaving right after a Rich Exit. However, my own experience does offer a number of learnings.

First year at Lucent/Bell Labs

Kenan Systems was one of several acquisitions Lucent made at the time. In the period they also acquired such rising stars as Ascend

Communications, Chromatis Networks, Nexabit Networks, and Ortel. Yet many of these acquisitions were soon withering under Lucent's command.

We were not.

Our product line continued its pre-Lucent growth curve as it continued rolling across the globe. In our first year with Lucent, we contributed 5 percent of the company's total net cash. This despite our now totaling 1,000 staff with the sales and marketing teams assigned to our product line, and Lucent's total staff numbering 135,000. We were, essentially, punching seven times above our weight.

Rather than having the easier workload I expected, I found the load only intensifying. So I bought a house in Summit to be closer to the office in Murray Hill, only a few miles away. Each morning I would try to stop by the first-floor museum of the Bell Labs facility— which also housed Lucent headquarters and where I was given a huge office—to marvel at all that Bell Labs had accomplished. Of course, I could never linger long. New history was being made on other floors in the building.

How Bell Labs really worked

Bell Labs was structured into two parts. There was a core of about a thousand scientists allowed to run "cage-free" and invent and innovate to their heart's desire. Funding for this group came from HQ and was determined by a percentage of revenue.

The second part, the Advanced Technologies unit, had about four thousand engineers and scientists who translated the inventions and innovations into real-world products for Lucent's five business units to sell.

While the corporation supported the Bell Labs staff directly, the Advanced Technologies unit was funded on a value-based arrangement. This was the perfect formula for discord, and early on we could plainly see the conflicts among all the internal groups playing out. It was strikingly similar to what I'd encountered between IT and end-users previously.

One time I was interested in test-driving some software that Bell Labs had produced. But one of the Lucent group presidents tried to warn me off, saying he didn't trust anything that came out of Bell Labs since their products were (a) often immature, (b) not easily implementable, and (c) slow to mature.

This kind of thinking from the business side floored me. I knew that several world-class software languages—including C++ and Unix—had been invented at Bell Labs. However, I also knew that the commercial benefits of those world-class products had accrued to others. Was it possible that the disconnects between Bell Labs and Lucent's business groups were part of the reason for that?

And could I solve for this apparent disconnect?

I thought about it a lot on my regular walks around Bell Labs. Possibly inspired by the very motto Lucent had adopted—*Bell Labs Innovation*—the proverbial light bulb went on one day. Why not hand-select fifty people from Kenan Systems, which I was still running, who knew how to move from innovation-to-implementation stage, and then hand-select another fifty from Bell Labs who brought deep expertise in software innovation, and create a composite unit that could rapidly go from inception to implementation to market?

Why not, I wondered.

I knew from Kenan Systems' transition from custom software maker to product maker that it was vital to keep the two groups as physically and organizationally separate as possible. I shared this thinking in operational terms with Lucent's CEO, Rich McGinn, and the Bell Labs president, Dan Stanzione.

They agreed to give it a try.

We used money from Kenan Systems' budgets, leased some space across the street, and moved a hundred people there. I named this new unit the Joint Development and Delivery Center (JDDC) so that any allegiances could be set aside, and the team could feel empowered to both develop and deliver valuable products. I also convinced the former branch manager of Kenan Systems' London office, John Rainger, to move to New Jersey to head up the JDDC.

If our new JDDC unit was going to succeed at each stage of bringing a product to market, we would need a framework that combined our telecom modules like billing, customer care, fraud detection, provisioning, etc., with an operating system that acted as the backbone. All the application modules would be sourced from Kenan Systems products, Bell Labs, as well as products from third-party vendors. Bell Labs would provide the operating system.

Bins, balls, and backplane

The framework was the thing. For JDDC to really succeed, I would need a framework that would capture the imagination of Lucent's higher-ups and a *vocabulary* to get it across effectively. I devised a framework and coined *Bins, Balls & Backplane*, *BBB* for short, to describe it.

- The *bins* would represent a bunch of things clustered together by their functional similarity, such as a bunch of different application modules (billing, provisioning, fraud detection, customer service, etc.);

- The *balls* would represent the individual applications being clustered;

- The *backplane* would be an operating system that tied the bins and balls together.

I mocked up a preliminary architecture for BBB and presented it to the key Lucent and Bell Labs executives. I launched into it with gusto, entirely ignoring the chuckles running around the table over the suggestiveness of bins and balls and backplane. Perhaps that innuendo made the BBB framework more memorable.

Progress on BBB was rapid.

It became a powerful innovation-to-implementation chain. In short order, we emptied out many of the reasonably mature software packages at Bell Labs and put them into the BBB platform.

And we began marketing our BBB, both as a total package and à la carte with just the applications the prospects wanted. BBB could then compete on price and on need.

With BBB, our JDDC unit became a translation and commercialization entity within Lucent/Bell Labs for the global telco market. With BBB, we were on our way toward revolutionizing the software underpinnings of the entire telecom industry.

Transitioning from CEO to subordinate

As year two neared, I expected big changes. I had agreed to one year as CEO, one year as ... something else. I was about to find out what that meant.

I prepared for my big meeting with the Communications Software Group president who I would now report to. But unexpectedly, he got fired. It was done, like so many firings at Lucent, by memo. Top management made the decision and announced it in an all-staff memo, using the typical line that he was leaving to pursue other interests.

So very different from how Kenan Systems had operated.

The COO at the time was Pat Russo. She tracked me down in Italy where I was pitching BBB to Telecom Italia after having pitched it to Deutsche Telekom. They were hot prospects for BBB.

Pat had called to offer me the job of group president of the Communications Software Group—my old boss's job!

Yes, I was surprised and favorably inclined. Perhaps foolishly.

I had no idea what I was getting into. I was soon thrust into the top executive team of Lucent, one of five group presidents. I inherited the legal, sales, HR, and operations infrastructure of a very large unit five thousand employees strong.

I was also, uncomfortably, the executive responsible for completing the integration of Kenan Systems into Lucent. That opened a big can of conflicting interests and loyalties, made more troubling by how little progress had been made in the first year toward melding the Kenan Systems culture with Lucent's own.

There I was, an academic and founder of a self-funded company that I grew based on a unique cultural, financial, and technology model ... thrust onto the highest tier of one of the largest public companies in the world, a company with a rich heritage, with the hottest IPO after the AT&T spinoff, with a stock that was widely held as a darling of Wall Street.

It was very demanding, very stressful.

Lucent's hyperaggressive sales model

At Kenan Systems our culture of caring about the health, well-being, and productivity of our people never once precluded making money.

We were laser-focused from day one on setting aggressive sales targets and then meeting them, and only feeling really good about ourselves if we blew right through those targets to new heights of profitability. Yet in my first meeting in year two with Lucent's CEO, he made it clear that my new sales targets had to increase twofold.

If the CEO could hear my pounding heart, he said nothing.

Instead, he explained how my unit's results would be included in the next quarterly reports to Wall Street and then onward for every quarter with ever-increasing revenue targets. And he informed me that I might be participating in earnings calls facing Wall Street analysts.

Doing the math quickly in my head, I couldn't see how we'd meet the super-aggressive growth targets. And so began a long run of sleepless nights, followed by long days of huddling with the company controller to prepare the quarterly financials, hobbled, in my mind anyway, by the discomfort that Lucent's accounting practices were, shall we say, novel.

Wall Street's quarterly orientation is a shocking thing to confront.

Back at Kenan Systems, we had always been conservative in our revenue recognition rules. That is, we used generally accepted accounting principles (GAAP) to book revenue when we earned it—meaning when we fulfilled our contractual obligations and the customer agreed as much. Traditional GAAP accounting has a whole lot of other rules and provisos that are more liberal.

Lucent approached it differently. Indeed, I was learning that many on Wall Street used liberal (creative?) accounting to basically construe revenue. One of the most egregious of them was Enron, and we know how that ended. *(Unfortunately, Lucent too would get entangled on this very issue later on.)*

But right then, the controller and I were at loggerheads. Accustomed to doing accounting by the book, I wanted to only report the revenue we'd earned in that quarter. But the controller wanted to include revenue that had been booked out into the future, which he said "should be considered sales" given the full value of the contracts even though the deliverables were way into the future.

Lucent was trying to wow Wall Street with impressive results, and I was trying to tamp down those results.

Worse, the Communications Software Group had been the worst-performing unit for a while. If I rejected some of the already-booked revenue, we'd fall further short of expectations.

Fortunately, the Kenan Systems product line was performing spectacularly. And we could carry those revenues into the current quarter. Our combined results painted a solid-enough bottom line that I was able to convince the controller to back out some of the revenue that would be disallowed under the conservative revenue recognition rules Kenan Systems was following.

Then came the sales model challenge.

Back at Kenan Systems and in my first year at Lucent, I had managed our sales force using a trusty triage mechanism. All leads came into marketing, then to be assigned by the small triage team to the salesperson best suited to call on the client. Plus, I reviewed the terms of each sales contract.

Very different from Lucent's MO.

While all five business groups had their sales targets set by the CEO, the actual sales themselves were made by a separate sales organization with its own empowered executive and its own marketing team, and to my surprise even its own technical development team meant to accelerate deliveries if the operating units were thought to be lagging.

Each of the business groups had to present their offers to the sales organization that went out and sold them. Usually, the most expensive offers were the switches—very complex, large-scale systems that did a lot of whirring and buzzing but essentially established a dedicated phone line between the caller and the receiver.

To close the sale on these expensive switches, salespeople often bundled in software products at little or no extra cost. It was good for goosing the revenue they could report, but not so good for the Communications Software Group, which was often left in the red as a result, and none too happy about it.

Meanwhile, those switches were going out the door at hefty prices, but at hefty cost of goods, as well as with slim margins. Software was just the opposite.

Tension rippled through the organization, exacerbated by externalities that were changing everything. The old world of voice calls was giving way to data (content) transmission. And those content calls were highly software dependent.

Seeing this trendline taking shape, I argued in management meetings that Lucent should give away voice but charge for data/content. I believed that Lucent could be a premier data transmission and storage company. Given that Lucent had command and control over the structure and architecture of the communication networks, it could have created a huge content-based business.

(*Cloud companies have that business now. Amazon is the biggest in this space with Amazon Web Services, which manages the content of Netflix and many others. It could have been Lucent doing that. And fair to say, as I was advocating, had Lucent management jumped to the fore of the content-based future of telecom, they might not have wound up merged into Alcatel SA of France a few years later. Perhaps wishful thinking on my part.*)

But back then, my arguments were met by blank stares, even hostility.

It had been far easier for a smaller company like Kenan Systems to react swiftly to, and even anticipate, changing markets. Now, in

Lucent's defense, they were trying to turn around an aircraft carrier in a tight channel. It was always going to be a challenge to meet the fast-changing markets. It had also been far easier to run sales and marketing at Kenan Systems and ensure that those customer-facing activities always remained consonant with our unique culture. I had long thought that customer should be spelled *custom-er ... the one that gives the company its customs or habits. If you have the wrong customers, the company culture and practices can only fall into dissonance.*

> *Custom-er ... the One That Gives Your Customs or Habits.*
> *Wrong Customers Lead to Bad Habits*

Previously the triage between leads and sales would allow for the ferreting out of leads that would not likely be good custom-ers. Now, that was not possible.

This point became starkly clear one day in my second year at Lucent. I was calling on a big telco customer that we'd acquired under Kenan Systems and brought over. I knew their executives well, and they had initiated the meeting. We had a delightful time of it, and productive too. Shortly after, I got an irate call from Lucent's head of sales. "Never should I call on *her* customers without *her* prior knowledge and consent," she told me in no uncertain terms.

Things were deteriorating fast.

Innovation backlog and the classical sales model

It had now become very clear why so many Bell Labs innovations never made it to market. Innovations are all about *future revenue*. But

Lucent's sales organizations were rewarded for *current revenue* or, even harsher, *quarterly revenue.*

Plus, the salespeople were assigned territories and were responsible for filling the lead funnel in those territories. Why would they take a chance on a risky offer that an innovative product often involves? Better to bank on the here and now, with products that are de-risked in the marketplace, and price acceptance good and established. Maybe, just maybe, if the lead funnel was empty, then they'd take a chance on a next-generation offer. That was the thinking in sales, naturally, because that was how the rewards system worked.

I could now clearly see why so many products didn't make it to market. And I began developing my own thinking on this, giving it a name—the innovation backlog. My new goal would be to try to solve for this backlog. *(We'll talk a little more about this here, and much more in the next book in this series.)* But right then, I had direct visibility into another key culprit in this nation's innovation backlog ...

> *Old-Style Territory-Based Find-and-Hunt Sales Models Contribute to the Innovation Backlog*

Next, running afoul of Lucent's lawyers

As group head, I was assigned a senior Lucent lawyer for drafting of contracts and the like. From the start, we were like the rowing teams I'd once watched from my office overlooking the Charles River, only with no coxswain and only left-side oars digging into the water.

Adding to the mix, Lucent's quasi-independent sales organization was ever ready to drill small holes in the boat if it meant a faster sale. That meant doing things like adding "most favored nation" clauses to sales contracts, which I then rejected and held my ground, but to little avail. Since the revenue of my group was in the hands of a distant sales force, they felt they could ignore me. And they did.

I did try to adapt to this new reality, I really did. But the clashes increased in both frequency and ferocity on three crucial fronts—in sales, in contracts, and in customer interactions.

And clearly something had to give.

I also knew, having taught some of the finest business minds in the country, that my own thoughts on these issues were entirely situational. That is, most large companies operated similarly to Lucent. I am not condemning Lucent or praising it. I was simply living a reality: if a founder wishes to stay on after the exit, or is required to stay on, best to be prepared for one jarring encounter after another.

Lucent's HR was hyperempowered

After so many scuffles with the lawyer and controller, it was no surprise when HR danced the same jig. I was president of a Lucent operating group, responsible for a good chunk of the company's earnings, but I had little to say about who worked with me.

Pretty much all hirings and firings, reviews and compensation packages, were in the hands of HR. Perhaps that was as it should be. But it had the effect of royally ticking off a lot of key people in companies Lucent had acquired. Not just our Kenan Systems people, but many more from the dozens of other acquired companies.

True or not, I was now learning how the big-company HR model also contributed to the innovation backlog.

Starting in the 1980s, many companies had reduced their R&D spending for a number of factors revolving around the globalization of the marketplace. The biggest trigger in many executives' minds was the "Japanese invasion." The island nation was delivering one new product after another with a speed of execution that few US companies could match. Feeling outgunned, US companies went on a buying binge. Acquiring companies—from technology startups to mature companies—in hopes of accelerating the introduction of new products.

This intense demand for acquisitions caused company valuations to skyrocket. Increases in company valuations across the decade varied widely across industries, but Thomson Reuters analysts concluded that M&A activity in the United States rose from $183 billion in 1990 to $1.7 trillion in 1999—a nearly tenfold increase. In the tech sector, the average price-to-earnings (P/E) ratio for publicly traded companies rose from fourteen in 1990 to seventy-three in 1999, according to Goldman Sachs.[20] Lucent was trading at a multiple of eighty. (They acquired Kenan Systems at a multiple of less than fifteen times KSC earnings. Indeed, the KSC transaction was six cents accretive to Lucent stock whereas the Ascend acquisition was six cents dilutive. Cleverly, both deals were announced back-to-back.)

Despite this sudden inflating of company values there seemed to be little concern and even less talk of a massive dotcom bubble burst that was hovering on the horizon.

As for Lucent, they were the biggest bull at the acquisition ball.

Seeing all this merger activity, it would've been clear to even a first-year business student that marriages that happen at the top can get shaky below. Two CEOs may have shaken hands, and teams of lawyers may have run up countless billable hours drafting the corporate marriage contract, but entities like IT, HR, sales and marketing, and production of the acquired and the acquirer rarely "marry," if ever.

As well, newly acquired companies bring their own customers—one of the big selling points. But now the acquirer has to manage a heterogeneous collection of customers. This could be difficult and add to the confusion and misunderstanding, causing many customers to walk if they could.

> *A Corporate Marriage Is Seldom Achieved Down the Hierarchy, Creating All New Problems*

As talent from the acquired companies make for the doors, and the previous customers do the same, the acquirer is left with only the technology they purchased. So, they end up paying a hefty premium for it. *(In my second book, we'll talk about a new model for mitigating this very real acquisition problem.)*

Lucent was facing all this in their thirty-plus acquisitions and problems were piling up like, well, big things piling up. And something had to give.

The big boardroom blowup

In October 2000, the Lucent Board met in Manhattan over the weekend. All five group presidents were there to make presentations. I again described *Bins, Balls & Backplane*—again to some chuckles. I also reported on another quarter of excellent results for my group.

Everything seemed hunky-dory.

On Monday I showed up for work, and like everyone else in the building I opened an all-company email. The Board had fired the CEO, presumably because Lucent had missed its earnings-per-share target. The chairman of the Board, Henry Schacht, was stepping in as acting CEO. A shocker, sure, but Lucent had a habit of firing executives on short notice.

Henry pulled a former COO, Bob Holder, out of retirement to be the COO once again. I didn't yet know what that'd mean for my group. But the corporate skies were clearly darkening, and more immediately, my two-year volunteer tour at Lucent/Bell Labs was ending in a few months.

Perhaps I could nominate one of my colleagues to take over? Who better than John Rainger, whom I'd hired a decade prior? He had been at HP, so he had big-company experience. He had superbly led Kenan Systems' expansion across Europe. He then headed JDDC, which was the true integration point of Kenan Systems and Bell Labs innovation.

I put the question to John. He said that the timing would have to be later in the spring so his wife could join him. I planned to nominate him right after Christmas.

Other events would come first.

Precipitated departure

By late 2000 it was clear that the initial promise of the Kenan Systems acquisition by Lucent, and all my hopes of transforming their business culture into one of innovation engineering, was stalling. I found myself arriving at work some days annoyed and frustrated—unusual for me. At one executive meeting, I finally blurted out ...

"This man falls 5,000 feet and nothing happens to him. And after a bit you'd have to say, 'Why, that's a miracle!' But then the man falls another foot and dies. In other words, what difference does it make if Lucent had been around for a century in various incarnations? There's an iceberg directly ahead. Captain, watch out!"

Perhaps I was seeing the iceberg more clearly as a former academic than the "seasoned" executives of Lucent did. Also, Kenan Systems had put the pedal to the metal for seventeen years and Lucent had acquired us precisely for that reason.

It was hard for me to watch, especially when business analysts began warning *en masse* that telecom and the dotcoms were on a collision course.

Rather than sit and shut up, I left for a long trip to Asia to drum up business. There were lots of opportunities for ARBOR and BBB and other products Kenan Systems had developed.

To harvest all the opportunities I was corralling, I proposed to Lucent that I return to the proven Kenan Systems sales model, hiring just ten people to execute on it. In return, I promised to deliver *much* higher sales volume—which struck me as an unassailable argument. I also repeated my request, based on my observations of commerce in Asia, that Lucent develop and offer content products that would be heavily software driven. In other words, migrate from hardware products to software offers. I even offered to test out all this within my own group, especially JDCC.

I met a wall of resistance.

Before long, the world would know Lucent was deep in financial difficulty.

My father used to say strong habits lie just below the soul. They do not depart until the soul departs. I suppose that deeply ingrained cultural habits and practices are part of the corporate soul. Until the corporation dies, or is near death, it is difficult to change.

As for me, there'd be no more change advocacy.

In early December, the COO Bob Holder called me in and indicated that I'd best leave. No reasons were given, except for vague words about me not fitting into the culture of Lucent. When I asked what that meant, he flat out said Lucent wouldn't tolerate me as a top executive.

That I didn't fit in the Lucent culture was yesterday's news. But an inability to tolerate me? Fair to say, I ran the wheel of emotional reactions to that. After cooling down, I met with Henry Schacht, the acting CEO, and he supported his COO's decision—as he should have, I suppose.

In parting, I tried to pass on some learnings, ever the lecturing professor.

I pointed out that Lucent had a small Board and that a larger Board might provide more support in critical times, and the stockholders might welcome more checks and balances, a variation on my classroom lecture on the hazards of unchecked CEOs. His response?

Stockholders can vote with their feet. If they don't like things, they can sell their shares and leave.

And so, in my leaving Henry's office for the final time, I was again struck by the threat of the overempowered CEO. With few checks and balances, CEOs can make big mistakes ... such as Lucent's arguably big role in the 2000 dotcom crash that took away 75 percent of NASDAQ investors' wealth.

In retrospect, I can see that I was indignant. Should I have been? My answer then was yes. Now I find it less wise. Old adage: he who gets up with anger sits down with loss. A new lesson learned: rather than getting indignant, which is a rather primitive reaction, a dialogue with a negotiation in mind would have been much better.

Negotiation-Oriented Dialog Rather than Indignation

Many times I have wondered if Bob Holder did me a great favor.

Within three years, Lucent's stock would tumble from its height of $80.00 to $0.50 a share, and from 135,000 employees to about

35,000. All this would have happened with or without me. The waves were colossal. However, had I not been "encouraged" to leave, I probably would have tried to soldier on, very likely without any meaningful impact, as the looming collapse was truly colossal and would have crushed me. Or at the least made me thoroughly frustrated day in and day out as I continued launching my pontifications—mere whispers in the tornadoes about to envelope not just Lucent but the whole of the telecom industry. But then the likes of JDDC and BBB might have been pivoting points for Lucent to transform itself.

So perhaps I owe Bob a thanks. Be that as it may, unfortunately, two decades later CEOs are even more empowered and untethered to systems of balance. And it represents an even greater threat to the corporate world and to our larger society, as well.

This is no longer just my own view, but one shared by many.[21]

On that cold day in late 2000, I returned to my office and fired off an email to all five thousand on my team. Yes, I would have preferred to speak with them face to face. But logistically it would be a mess. I told them I was leaving forthwith—a few months ahead of schedule. And that was that.

For days into weeks, I would reflect on the COO's words, "Do you really think Lucent would have someone like you as a top executive?" I had no idea what it really meant, other than it was obviously hurtful. That hurt would be slow to wear off, but it would in time and then some insight would emerge.

Years later, I ran into a Lucent Board member in a social setting. He casually mentioned that my name had surfaced as a possibility when they were hunting for a new CEO way back in 2000 after McGinn was fired and Schacht had stepped in as acting. Sure, it was not unusual for a company like Lucent to consider internal candidates.

But me, with all my academic baggage and infuriatingly long lectures, as someone had put it?

Apparently, I was one of the finalists nominated by the search committee. Was that what Bob was getting at? I would not be tolerated as a top executive—that is, the CEO. I will never know, and truly it is irrelevant. If our paths do cross, I am inclined to thank him for precipitating my departure. For if left to my means, I might have hung around far too long and become a helpless executive watching a hundred-plus-year powerhouse crumble into history and inclined to tell all kinds of Hodja stories but without many getting amused.

Instead, I went on to the next massive project of validation of a different kind—to be described in the next book.

In time, Lucent disbanded our JDDC operation. But Balls, Bins & Backplane (BBB) lives on in business theory, or so I like to think. Look at your iPhone or iPad. There it is. You can put the Balls (which are the apps) into the Bins (which you can name Entertainment, Travel, Office, etc., or Apple will name them for you) and the Bins and Balls plug into the Backplane (the operating system iOS).

No doubt a case of co-invention.

Also living on is ARBOR. It was renamed Kenan/BP by Lucent shortly after I left, presumably because Kenan Systems had earned a place for itself in the business ecosystem. Amdocs would later buy Kenan/BP and not only retain the name but build up revenues topping $5 billion from processing more than a billion telco subscribers globally—a third of the total market.

It is gratifying knowing that my old classroom pontifications had gotten the validation I was seeking. Kenan Systems transformed so much of the software industry and our crowning achievement—ARBOR, then Arbor/BP, now Kenan/BP—has become the backbone of telcos across the world. And of course, these telcos are the backbone of the internet. And arguably, Kenan/BP is a huge success story for AI, as it was then.

I set out to prove a framework built from many first principles and learnings that aspiring entrepreneurs could use to their great advantage in creating a Lean Startup and transforming it into a successful Lean Company that is well poised for a Rich Exit.

I believe that our sensational team succeeded in that.

And Kenan Systems earned a place for itself in the business ecosystem, including a Harvard Business School case, even if Kenan Sahin was now unemployed.

9

VALIDATION, ALL OVER AGAIN

A man sets out to seek the meaning of life. He visits a monk who tells him to drink a magic tea, and all will be revealed. He drinks the tea. He goes to bed. He wakes up the next morning and feels no different, has no insights. He tells the monk as much. The monk replies, "So what?" A bit perturbed, the man asks, "Now what?" And the monk says, "Yes, that's the meaning of life: 'so what' and 'now what.'"

And that's where I was. Wondering … shrugging off the past as "so what?" Let the past be past. What is in the future, the "now what"?

A thousand cups of tea couldn't have prepared me for how that question would be answered.

With Lucent now behind me, my wife and I were settling into a townhouse on Beacon Hill and taking it easy. One day over a leisurely breakfast reading the *Boston Globe*, a story leaped out that just broke my heart. The once shining star in technology innovation, Arthur D. Little, Inc. (ADL) was having serious problems after 116 years of operations.

It was even sadder coming on the heels of so many corporate declines. Not just Lucent/Bell Labs. Also such luminaries as Digital

Corp, Polaroid, Kodak, RCA, and Sarnoff. The torrent waters of the 1990s left only a few companies untouched.

But ADL? Oh, it had a place in my heart!

ADL was founded in 1886 by Arthur Little and was perhaps the country's longest-running technology generation and consulting company. It would give us a rich legacy of commercializing innovations. And it would be bequeathed by Mr. Little to MIT upon his death in 1935. MIT would run it until the 1950s. Under MIT stewardship, ADL would develop synthetic penicillin, cryogenics, novel desalinization. When it was spun off as an employee-owned company (an ESOP), it would continue that innovation heritage. Out of ADL would come the venerable Boston Consulting Group and from that, Bain & Co. Fine organizations, all.

Ever the unreformed professor, I set out to meet ADL's CEO and share my hopefully helpful learnings from over the years. And in turn, to get the CEO's insights and perspectives for a book I was contemplating writing.

I wrote a long letter, proposing to meet.

No response came back.

A few weeks later, another *Boston Globe* story told that ADL had filed for bankruptcy. It was now apparent why the CEO hadn't responded. Oh well, I thought, and moved on.

But my letter did not!

The firm that was handling the restructuring of ADL called one day to say (a) they had seen my letter, (b) the bankruptcy judge had rejected a Chapter 11 reorganization and instead ordered a Chapter 7 liquidation, which meant (c) ADL would be auctioned off in sixty days in five lots, one being the Technology and Innovation unit and (d) would I be interested in buying any of it?

I told him I was the wrong person, and merely wanted to learn more since I was planning a book on R&D. He invited me to New York.

There I learned all about the bankruptcy and liquidation. But my real interest was the "classic ADL." That was ADL's Technology and Innovation unit (T&I as it was known) with some fifty labs and 250 highly trained professionals, many graduates of Harvard, MIT, Stanford, etc. The restructuring firm told me I could have access to the T&I data room, but only if I submitted a bid to buy. Apparently some thirty big-name companies were interested in T&I and were doing their due diligence right then. If I wanted in, I'd have to join them, at least so I understood or perhaps so construed what was said.

The idea of laying my own eyes on the inner workings of so much historical data and so many distinguished people—well, it really got its hooks into me. Why not submit a bid?

The probability of my bid even being considered would have to be zero. And in the meantime, I could access this rich body of data and even interview the bidding companies to gain insights into their due diligence. It sounded like a perfect project for a man with suddenly a lot of time on his hands.

I went to my lawyers for advice in proceeding. That they thought I was crazy was obvious in their expressions. Only three weeks to pull a bid together, and without any due diligence? Totally insane!

I explained my logic. There were thirty companies doing due diligence, so there was no chance my bid would be seriously considered. On that basis, I formed a company named TIAX LLC and through it placed a bid of around $15 million—a made-up number, a placeholder.

While the legal wheels turned, I jumped gleefully into downloading a hard drive full of data on T&I's internal processes and operations over the years. I felt like a Boston hockey fan riding a Zamboni down center ice, I was so happy.

Come April 4, 2002, they held the auction at the Beacon Hill offices of the law firm of Goodwin Proctor, near my residence on the "flat" of Beacon Hill. So I went, if only to interview some of the big-name bidders. More material for the book I still planned on writing.

But the halls did not present any roaming executives for me to interview. Yes, there were some, but they were seeking the other four parts of ADL. Shortly before 7 p.m. we filed into the auction room. At the appointed hour the auctioneer began with T&I announcing that there had been only *one* bidder for it … TIAX. Going once, going twice, *sold*.

I was dumbfounded. Maybe I still am.

It turned out the placeholder price of $15 million was way too high but it was pivotal. Apparently, the ADL bankruptcy was triggered because they could not pay a $70 million loan from the private equity firm Cerberus (after the mythological three-headed dog that guards hell—what a name!). So that was the so-called "stalking horse" bar that had to be exceeded for the auction to take place. The bidders for the other four parts had come in low, and why not? It was an auction after all, where further bidding was expected. And since the TIAX bid was high enough that when combined with the other bids just exceeded the bar, the auction could take place. Otherwise, the three-headed dog that guarded hell in mythology would have walked away with all of ADL. At the end, the auction netted around $95 million with $15.4 coming from TIAX, meaning me. That turned out to be just the beginning.

"Me" would eventually put in nearly $100 million and have no regrets.

Coming home to my wife, Andrea, late that night (1 a.m. or so) and waking her up gently, sheepishly I said, "Dear, remember the trips we were planning across the world? Well, on Monday I go to work as head of TIAX with 250 employees I've not met except a few senior people on the only visit I made to the ADL campus at Alewife in Cambridge. Uh, sorry."

After her shock wore off, she admitted to knowing that sooner or later I'd get into trouble. This qualified as sooner. How fortunate I was to have her support. She deserved—we both deserved—some restful time together.

But it would have to wait.

Four days later, bright and early, I reported to work and called a team meeting. No longer the guy on the Zamboni, I was now the cowboy riding into Dodge City on a mule with two rusty pistols, declaring I'm here to save Dodge! Imagine the amazement of these accomplished talents staring back at me. They probably thought the old man's lost it.

Nonetheless I dove into some after-the-fact due diligence to suss out what I'd acquired. I had 250 world-class talents with quite the payroll, and business on the books for 150 of them at best. Clearly there was a good reason the company had been liquidated, and nobody at auction for this unit except the accidental and naïve participant—TIAX. The unit was worth far less than my $15 million placeholder.

In the first team meeting on April 10, 2002, I declared a *no* layoff and *no* salary-cut policy. I also told them that I held none of the hidden objectives their clever minds were surely conjuring up. I was there not as an investor but to work alongside them as a member of this new company, TIAX.

Listening to myself speak, I wouldn't have believed in me. Credibility lower than whale's poop, as the wags say. Why would anybody put up so much money and not expect a return?

But there I was.

This cowboy soloing it on a mule, and not about to turn back.

It was time to begin anew, to start all over again with a broken company in need of restoration. And to figure out how to restore it to compete in a new century with the kind of organizational structure now called for.

New ideas and perspectives would be required.

Oh yes, I was excited. Another way to validate classroom teachings and learnings, confirm Kenan Systems' framework with its first principles, debunk some, and validate others but now in a restart of one of the most important heritage companies in the United States, with restoration as the guiding strategy, a company that shared a lot with Bell Labs. Were the mythological muses inspiring me or just having fun with me by putting me on a journey that is still continuing after twenty-one years?

So where from here?

There is so much more to be said about restoring and elevating the potential of great American companies.

And the art of business restoration.

A strong hand is needed to rescue a business in trouble, preserving its foundational expertise while jettisoning the strictures preventing it from succeeding in today's economy.

Dismantling a troubled company is surely not always the best turnaround strategy. Indeed, the art of the restoration begins, as on a painter's canvas, with an eye to what should be left in and what left out. From these decisions come the first insights into whether the traditional Turnaround Model, or a Restoration Model, is more ideally suited to transforming the company.

Embedded in the Restoration Framework (subject of the next book) is a critical transformational strategy I call *Change but No Change*. It is, I believe, an effective way to surmount a looming obstacle, which is this: a company long steeped in its own culture is only able to change when there appears to be no change at all.

Perhaps you sense the beauty of this strategy?!

APPENDIX A: A GIFT AND LETTERS LOOKING BACK

As we transitioned from the COVID-19 pandemic year of 2020 to yet another pandemic year of 2021, I was looking forward to a very special day, March 31, when I would become eighty, but still feeling much younger. Of course, with the pandemic still raging there would be no parties and gifts would be dropped off at doorsteps.

That's when my son Kent surprised me with a most ingenious gift: a Zoom call on my birthday with those who had worked at Kenan Systems. Wow. He had set up a website and coordinated the call with some of the "old crew." To my utter amazement, close to 150 of them signed up for it—including some of our first hires. In fact, Darren Walsh agreed to be the moderator. How appropriate for the staunch keeper, teacher, and promoter of the Kenan Systems way.

At the appointed hour, there I was back in the old days, as though conducting a staff meeting. It was so real and I felt like I was transported back in time. That wonderful gift from Kent gave me the closure that I'd missed when I so suddenly departed from Lucent on that bleak December day in 2000. Better late than never.

As part of the event, I received testimonials that speak to the exceptional people I was able to work with, and so grateful to have them as friends, then, now, and always. And I am very confident that they will continue to apply and propagate the principles we all forged together across multiple decades. What a ride.

A few of the testimonials came as direct emails to me. Most came as a compendium Sharon Lowe had assembled for a presentation on the birthday Zoom.

Here are a few of the ones that came directly. I chose them for their relevance to the points in the book—though I appreciated each and every one I received. They were uniformly heartwarming.

Selected direct letters

From Eric Wheatley, who is clearly carrying on the torch at Amdocs, the only worthy competitor we had. So it is fitting that Arbor/BP renamed Kenan/BP and FX are at Amdocs. If Eric had not mentioned that over a billion subscribers are on these platforms employing fourteen hundred people globally, I would not have known. Even more gratifying.

> *From: Eric Wheatley*
> *Date: March 31, 2021 9:51:47 AM EDT*
> *Subject: Happy 80th Birthday, Dr. Sahin!*

As the current stewards of the Kenan/FX and Kenan/BP revenue management solutions, the employees of Amdocs salute you and wish you a happy 80th birthday!

The software assets created on your watch are still evolving, in daily use by over 1 billion subscribers and are the primary source of employment for nearly 1,400 people globally.

The success of what you created continues, and we are grateful for the opportunity to carry the legacy forward.

Wishing you many more years of health and prosperity.

All the best from the managers and employees of Amdocs Optima—the current home of the assets originating with Kenan Systems Corporation.

From Keith Sawyer, who was critical to the success of the Citi-Expert project and also of ARBOR's early versions. When he told me he was departing to pursue his PhD, I could only be encouraging. He is now a distinguished professor and authority on innovation, among other topics, with more than a dozen books published. The letter below is an abbreviated version, as all letters are, so that only the relevant parts are included.

Dear Kenan,

It was great to see you at your birthday Zoom event. I remember well those times in the 1980s that you talked about in the Zoom meeting—when we did CitiExpert ... and then went to US West and we created ARBOR, which was then just an expert system for repairing bills and service order requests ...

When I left Kenan Systems, in 1990, the company was still almost exclusively a [custom software] consulting firm, and I'm impressed with the transition to a product company when ARBOR was transformed into a full billing system. Because I left, I missed a chance to grow with the company, but you know of the joys of the academic life, and going to graduate school was a good choice for me. I've been a productive scholar and I've reached my dream job as an endowed professor at a top research university.

You were a wonderful mentor and I learned very much from our frequent flights on the shuttle. Years later, I told everyone that when you add all of our flights together, I got as much education as an entire two-year MBA program. In fact, I used a lot of that knowledge when I taught in the executive education program at Washington University's Olin School of Business ... My workshops drew on my research on how to build a collaborative creative culture and how to lead innovative teams. I got high ratings and kept getting invited back each year ... I couldn't have provided true value to those executives without the experience I got working with you.

With best wishes,

Dr. R. Keith Sawyer

Morgan Distinguished Professor in Educational Innovations,

University of North Carolina at Chapel Hill

From Carol Levasseur, a distinguished member of the legal team at Kenan Systems and later at Lucent. She and I confronted a huge number of clients and almost always ended up with clean, fair, and mutually beneficial "peace" contracts.

Dear Kenan,

It was so nice to see and hear from you at your Zoom birthday party! You haven't changed one bit and if I didn't know better I would swear we were all back 20+ years ago at a company meeting. I know I'm not alone when I say the Kenan Systems days were the best years of my career. So much excitement, so much work but so much fun and so many very talented people who to this day feel a strong connection to one another. As the younger people say these days, "if you know, you know."

My son, Christian, who is now 21 and is graduating from Dartmouth College this June, has heard all my Kenan stories and is always amazed when he mentions a company and I say I know a senior person who works there—of course it's always a former Kenan person. If Christian had ever asked to speak with someone I know at one of those companies, I would have had no qualms about reaching out regardless of how long it had been since we had spoken because you know you can always contact a fellow Kenanite!

When he was deciding whether to take [an] offer over some other opportunities at larger … companies, my advice was to take this position where he was given so much autonomy and the ability to work with a team he genuinely likes and respects.

My advice was coming directly from my experience at Kenan Systems. If Christian can have a similar experience to mine at Kenan Systems I will be so happy for him.

I miss you, Kenan, and those days at Kenan Systems and I'm so happy to see you happy and as enthusiastic as ever. Happy birthday and wishing you many more to come.

Regards,
Carol Levasseur

From Sharon Lowe, another star to join our Washington, DC, office in documentation and move superbly into marketing and become the master of so many areas. She was a model AAWE.

Believe it or not, in my current role with Amdocs (yes, I am still with Kenan) I do a lot of special projects around community building: presentations, newsletters, videos, websites, etc. It is the less serious part of my job but one I enjoy.

KSC was for me—as with many—perhaps the most important professional learning experience of our careers. Yes, we were all very young. But moreover, you built and encouraged an environment where any individual would be heard no matter what their job title. Ideas were important; who your boss was didn't matter. Everyone could have as much responsibility as they could handle (honestly, probably a little more than that). KSC created leaders, not managers. Everyone was smart and hardworking … and did NOT take themselves too seriously. I worked harder at KSC than I have in my career since …

I remember one day making some impassioned argument to you and your response was, "True, but unimportant." I could try to count the many times I have passed that one on, but better to tell you that my 19-year-old told me the other day that he says it all the time.

From Mark Friedman, who ably headed and expanded marketing globally, which encompassed Client Success Management and Partner Development. In his note below he captures our commitment to client success at times ignoring client satisfaction; and also marketing owning the leads.

Kenan, you are a great inspiration—and someone who taught and developed me tremendously. I apply so many of your lessons to this day and remain deeply appreciative: Market Development ("Mark, let's build a model where our sales team works only on leads developed by Market Development—and our salespeople will love it!"), Partner Development ("Mark, this will be key to our Product-centric model"), and Client Success (only Kenan can look 100s of customers in the eye with a smile and say "we don't care about your satisfaction" followed by a long pause and then say … "we care only about your success—and sometimes we will know better than you will what to do to succeed!" and have those 100s of customers smile with him!).

⸻

From Aidan Lloyd, the Harvard grad who loved C++ utility development and was exceptional at it; however, he was not at all interested in interacting with customers. He once asked me, "Do people really enjoy that kind of stuff?" Did he go to the wrong school in Cambridge?

My favorite Kenan corny story literally involves corn. A farmer wants to reward a helper's hand and allows him to pick his amazing corn, the best in the valley, but some conditions:

1. you're standing at the edge of a cornfield

2. you're handed an empty bushel basket

3. you're allowed to walk into the cornfield in any direction

4. you're not allowed to change direction

5. as long as you have room left in your basket, you can pick an ear of corn and place it in the basket

The person begins his walk noting each ear of corn is better than the one before. Keeps going to make sure his basket has absolutely the best ears only. Suddenly he is at the end and his basket is empty. The moral: you could identify the best but if they don't go into your basket you end up empty-handed.

(My note: I used to tell the story that in making selections, it is better to go for the excellent and grab it rather than trying to find the best. Yes, you can find the best of the lot but will it still be there for you to have? A corollary: the best of average is still average, underscoring the point that the real search criterion is not the "best" but "excellent." Spot excellent, and grab it before others do!)

———————

From Mike Cebry, the great architect of Hourglass that became a backbone of KSC, and of META that became a backbone of USPS and later a huge revenue source for ADL. Ironically, years later, I would continue my validation journey with the "classical" ADL.

It was truly a pleasure to share in your 80th birthday celebration. So many memories of talented people doing innovative and amazing things. Thank you for the opportunity you gave me to be a part of such a unique and special company, and the coaching along the way.

- Your trust in me to chair the compensation committee ("We can rotate the leader from Mike Cebry to Cebry, Mike")

- Your advice to find a role that fits your aptitude/attitude when I was choosing between Arbor/BP consultant or Manager Special Projects ("You can make a rabbit try to climb a tree, but he is happier running fast on the ground"—or something to that effect).

- And all the Kenan-wide practices—agile software development approach, AAWE hiring, dynamic reconfiguration, etc., etc.

———————

Selections from the testimonials compendium

While I thoroughly enjoyed every one of the dozens and dozens of testimonials and remembrances from the days at Kenan Systems, I have selected a few that relate directly to the points in the book, abbreviating them to highlight the relevant points with some added contextual comments.

Darren Walsh
1983-2006 Cambridge, Denver Development, Consulting CEO

... If you want to get to the moon, you can't keep walking up the mountain. You keep getting closer but stop when you reach the top. It requires new thinking. You have to travel back down the mountain, build a rocket ship, and continue on your journey from there ... Here I am sitting at my desk in 1984 [the picture omitted] not realizing I'd be here for another 24 years ...

(Darren was the custodian of the Kenan Systems culture as well as the key enhancer and promoter of it. He established our training academy in Denver that became the training ground for staff from around the world. He was one of the robust pillars of Kenan Systems and the leader of its consulting arm. He joined as one of the six part-timers in the summer of 1983 and stayed on for twenty-four years, even longer than I did!)

Ramón Bueno
1985-2006 Cambridge Consulting

Kenan's proverbial anecdotes at general meetings to make a point about design guidelines, practical advice, etc. (e.g., at a progress update presentation to a client, not starting with all the things that still don't work; or illustrating a point starting with an estimate of the # of atoms in the universe, or walking through a cornfield ...). The many years we worked collegially in small teams finding good (sometimes even elegant) solutions to decision-making systems challenges, without the rigidity common to many organizations. ACUMATE (never saw anything quite like it again).

(Ramon was truly a "bueno" colleague in so many ways and applied the Kenan Systems principles and vocabulary ably. He notes the importance of NOT starting with confessions, the cruelty of combinatorial complexity, the use of "excellence" rather that the "best" for selection, teaming of teams, and collegial socialization to find solutions. As he notes, ACUMATE was a remarkable development language way ahead of its time. It handled multidimensions well and as such was a nice fit for the Kenan Systems multidimensional structure.)

Kent Sahin
1982–2001 DC, Cambridge Marketing, Sales CEO
of REAL Software Systems, Needham, MA

Kenan Systems was a playground we all built a city around, and the fun, optimism, and belief in the goodness of people remained intrinsic to its heart and soul. I had a pretty unique experience at Kenan Systems ranging from cleaning out offices as a kid to entertaining and negotiating with CIOs in later years. I cherish the deep sense of pride we all had in the quality of our work and the unflappable ethics of the Kenan Systems community. Also, the course we all took from Prof. Kenan in Applied Analogies has been very useful.

(As I mention in the book, Kent was my son but not recognized as such by most clients and even staff. People thought "Kenan" was my last name and hence Kenan Systems. I was often addressed as Mr. Kenan. Kent went on to expand on the Kenan Systems models and learnings to found REAL Software, which he grew to be an international company in the IP management space in seven different industry sectors. In so many ways he provided an independent validation of what this book describes as a framework for Lean Startup to Lean Company to Lean Exit. Had he chosen to continue with his company a few more years, he would have come close to a super-rich exit à la Kenan Systems but he achieved a richer exit by balancing personal and professional lives—the balance I found eventually.)

Nan Solomons
1996–2000 Cambridge Office Support and Implementation
Faculty, University of New England, Portland, ME

… Risk was encouraged, fear was not … AAWE is the optimal hiring approach … At the time I was looking for a new job, I said that I wanted a place where employees read the New Yorker *and watched foreign films. I got that, along with lifelong friends and acquaintances.*

(Nan captures the essence of Kenan Systems well: it was a safe environment for the staff and for me as well. I shared all kinds of thoughts without fear, as I was a colleague who also worked for the company. With the AAWE way of hiring, it was essential to have that safe environment for the new hires to learn, master, practice, and teach in a record time. And also have fun. We all had fun. An old proverb: if you don't want to work, find a job you like. I for sure did not feel like I was working, especially in the later years.)

Amy Kirschenbaum Swers
2000–2002 Miami, Buenos Aires Market Development

Kenan Systems gave me my first big break as a professional. It is one of my favorite stories. I was called for an initial interview in error (campus recruiters were seeking engineers, but somehow this political science major was contacted). Kenan Systems was a company that believed in the liberal arts college philosophy and my ability to learn the job. The company was filled with remarkable colleagues, many of whom I consider friends to this day …

(Amy might have thought it was an error but when it was Aptitude and Attitude and Willingness to Learn we valued, she clearly was the right candidate. She accurately captures the broad way of thinking that pervaded the company, which allowed the iterative blending through socialization of diverse perspectives that led to creative solutions (actually resolutions) that made the impossible possible. I used to joke that we do the impossible in a few days; miracles take a little longer. With such an amazing staff, that corny saying often turned out to be so.)

Bill Hobbib
1998–2001 Cambridge Marketing

Teaming of teams. There aren't good events or bad events; they're just events. When your workload increases, you need to apply compression techniques so you can get everything done. Hiring model based on aptitude, attitude, willingness to learn, and experience made for an amazing culture—one unlike any other I've been a part of. I've practiced and preached that same hiring model over and over in every company I've been at. But Kenan did it best.

(Bill was an excellent student and a practitioner of the Kenan Systems principles that he augmented by reading relevant articles and books. I am glad he has highlighted *teaming of teams*, a topic I would dwell on extensively but did not get to discuss in this book. I would often opine that we, from our early schooling on, learn to operate in teams, which then compete. That early training hinders teaming of teams in the work environment. So I would encourage team leaders to Learn & Teach the *teaming of teams*. Bill also brings up *compression*. I would often point back to the college student days of taking courses, having extracurricular activities, and having a personal life being possible only by mastering *compression*. Why not practice that at work? Pile it on and get it done. How? With compression. And as in so many of the testimonials, Bill points out it was the AAWE approach of hiring and of course the sequel, focusing on staff development combined with Teach & Learn, Learn & Teach, that made Kenan Systems so successful.)

Emily (Zarins) Mason
1998–2001 Cambridge Marketing Amgen in Thousand Oaks, CA

... Old hat, new hat ... The camaraderie was really special, both within Marketing and also across departments. Also, I vividly remember seeing the Lucent acquisition posted on the door when we came in the day of the announcement. As an M&A lawyer, I always keep this experience in mind, including what Kenan accomplished to take care of employees and the company post-acquisition.

(I did commit to two years to Lucent, wanting to make the transition to the legendary telco and innovation hub smoother. How could one anticipate these two combined giants collapsing in just three years after having been in business for over a hundred years? Good news—Kenan Systems survived the collapse of not just Lucent and Bell Labs but of the entire dotcom ecosystem and now Arbor/BP or Kenan/BP services has more than 30 percent of telco subscribers. All because of the commitment of Emily and so many of our other staff buttressed by the strong structural framework of Kenan Systems.)

Shey (Shetal) Mistry
1998-2004 London Consulting Director of Bruhati in the UK

... If you drop a pebble in the middle of the pond and you wait, then the ripples will eventually move across the whole pond ... Amazing people and culture. I'm still in touch with many colleagues and many of whom I consider my closest friends. I still fondly remember all of the travel around the world and working at many Telco operators with other Kenanites from local offices. I started at Kenan Systems as a graduate and left six years later with a vast amount of experience and knowledge in a short space of time. CITC in Denver was the best training course I've ever attended to date! It was always a lesson in life listening to Kenan's stories in the London office; what an amazing teacher and visionary!

(I used to bring up pebbles and ponds to drive home that a slight change in the program could have ripples across the whole system and it might be a while before the ripples are detected. I am humbled by Shey's description of me. Yes, I was a teacher but so were the staff. We learned and taught and vice versa. And of course there was the formal teaching at CITC that Darren had set up. I think every startup at one point should codify its principles and vocabulary and set up a CITC.)

Caroline Kerrigan
1998-2000 Cambridge and Rio de Janeiro Consulting
Harvard Pilgrim HealthCare Institute Favorite

... Money is an enabler ... The versatility of the product ... I was able to do freelance consulting in Paris, Prague, and Wellington (New Zealand) because of the skills I gained on consulting projects.

(Full version: money is an enabler like the power in an outlet. It is the appliances that plug into the outlets that create value. At Kenan Systems we built the equivalent of appliances, but money had to be there for what we built. Caroline also highlights the portability of the skills learned, a key learning at Kenan Systems being *skillful repurposing.*)

Olivier Suard
1997-2000 London Sales and Marketing VP Marketing

… Kenan wearing an "umbrella hat" to illustrate the importance of understanding what customers actually want.

(Another principle not discussed in the book directly, and remembered by the team because I would sometimes wear an umbrella hat that I purchased in China for one dollar. So in principle, there is an executive who wants to buy hats for a function. He wants the hats to be wind and rain resistant, provide sun protection, and be cheap. The salesperson, excited to have found the right hat, presents an umbrella hat. But the executive is not pleased. He forgot to mention one key criterion that the hats be fireproof. "What?" the salesman protests. The reason is not fireproofed hats; the exec wants his staff to look good. But that is not a legitimate criterion. The lesson: don't be swayed by the specs articulated. Learn to read thoughts. A variant of what I learned from Avery Johnson.)

Felicita Stone
1999-2005 Miami Technical Training,
Marketing Development & Sales

Twenty-one years later, I still think my time in Kenan was one of the most rewarding professional experiences in my career.

(I continue to be amazed and delighted that for so many of the staff, the Kenan Systems experience remains a standout even after decades and across many companies. Imagine my surprise that on my 80th, 150 staff would sign up for the Zoom even though I had left Kenan Systems twenty years ago. I attribute most of that to the Kenan Systems framework, held together by a rich set of principles and our dedication to making a difference without ever compromising ethics.)

Rosangela Souza
Ten years Rio Operations, Living in Rio

... Friday breakfast and L&L (Lunch and Learn)—I still am missing this ... Nice thing about Kenan (the company) is that we still meet each other and we still feel like Kenanites.

(I too miss L&L. They were fun with both the mind and the body nourished. Rosangela highlights the bonding that the Kenan Systems culture and framework created that continues among the *Kenanites*.)

Andrew D'Souza
1998-2007 DC Consulting

It's not about the money; it is about making a difference. The collegial/ collaborative culture ...

(Indeed, we focused on the success of our clients and making a difference for the industries we served—at times displeasing them along the way. And money followed. At the time of the Lucent transaction Kenan Systems had achieved 50 percent cash margins without focusing on *maximizing* margins. We *satisficed* meaning balancing many objectives. The culture was collegial because we had wholesale imports from academia as part of this big multidecade experiment in validation.)

Doug Zone
1997-2001 Cambridge, Bracknell, London, Singapore, Madrid Partner Management, Product Management

... I can hear Kenan's voice to this day, but the exact words escape me ... Something he said to me over dinner in Madrid about not working so hard but, please, keep working hard.

(Doug was key to the success of our Madrid office, which serviced Telefonica and its reach into Latin America. He too was an AAWE hire from Sloan and was able to multitask very ably. What Doug touches on is a reflection on my learning early on that for each adage that says do this there is another that preaches the opposite. In my academic training I learned that dynamic systems, especially the biological ones, operate by balancing the *do* with the *don't*—for example, sleep and/or be awake or the proverbial fight and/or flee. Hence my paradoxical comment to Doug. The resolution to this dilemma is *context*. Nighttime is a good context to fall asleep but driving is NOT.)

Will Rotch
1989-2012 Cambridge USPS, Acumate, Strategist, Presales Consulting

... At a company meeting, when pressed hard on why we don't have employee ownership of the company: "Really this is just a piece of paper. It's hard to put a value on it—it doesn't mean much."

(Will was another key person who ably stepped into many roles. His knack for adding many, many words to a point in some ways allowed noisy exploration. In the book I touched on restricted stock but the more common vehicle is stock options and that came up many times, especially in recruiting. Here is how I would approach it. Typically companies that give stock options benefit in two ways: they take a tax deduction on the presumed value even though options are not tradable and they pay below market, as the options are deemed to be part of the compensation. A really attractive candidate hesitated to join us even though he really liked us because we did not offer options. He had a competing offer in hand. I made our offer and then asked him what salary he was offered by the other company. As I expected, it was well below our offer. So I asked who was paying for the options. He was puzzled. I pointed out that actually he would be financing the other company with the difference between the pay they offered and his true market value. In fact, he would be taking two chances: joining a startup and then in reality investing in the same company. Why not take our offer at (above) market, take the salary difference, and invest it in a secure portfolio? He still seemed hesitant but wanted to discuss it with his wife. He did, then accepted our offer and became an excellent employee. The reality is, many employees who join because of options really do not stay long enough to benefit from those options. A bird in hand ...)

Steve Allor
1997–2001 Cambridge Global Partner Program,
NA Field Marketing, Offer Management

... *"Steve, could you come to my office and spend some time with [this executive from far far away] and share with them our Partner Strategy ... and I will [not] be right back!"* ... *"Do you blow on yogurt because you were once burnt by hot milk?"*

(Steve, an excellent AAWE recruit from HBS, together with Mark, really extended our Partner Program to make it global. What he describes is a method I would use to show to executives how capable our staff were. I would leave a colleague, who had barely been with us a year, alone with a client executive to, for instance, give a demo. Then upon rejoining, I would point out that the colleague had just recently joined us to highlight a) what quick learners our staff were and b) how easy it is to learn and demo our systems. As to the yogurt, that was an adage from my childhood days: he who gets burned from hot milk tends to blow on yogurt. Or put another way: our early trauma can, if unchecked, make us risk averse.)

Rob Glover
1988-2014 Cambridge, DC, Denver
Development—USPS to Arbor/BP

I spent some time in Lithuania on one of our first Arbor/BP deployments. This was about one year after their independence. It was fascinating to see their reimagining of society after decades of Soviet control … Friends who felt like family, Friday afternoon socials, building and delivering amazing software.

(Rob was the ultimate in versatility and adaptability. He successfully moved from office to office, country to country. What he describes for Lithuania happened in many countries that became independent after the collapse of the Soviet Union, as they embraced consumer-oriented capitalism to which pricing is key. Arbor/BP with its detailed billing provided that pricing mechanism in that central area: telecommunications, without which markets cannot function. The fact that Arbor/BP could be deployed for millions of subscribers right out of the box, and on inexpensive minicomputers as opposed to years for custom systems on cumbersome mainframes, was an enabler of democratic capitalism as it marched into the formerly Soviet-controlled nations.)

Carolina Moya Lisamore
2001-20015 Miami Consulting

... My gratitude to Kenan for the legacy that is reflected in the lives of all the colleagues that passed by Kenan Systems. I joined in 2001 and made friends for life.

(Because I left in December of 2000, I did not get to meet Carolina but we clearly met through the bonding that Kenan Systems created for all of us. Let me just conclude these testimonials by indicating that even as these amazing colleagues show their gratitude, I have even more gratitude for each and every one of them.)

As this book tries to articulate, and all these testimonials have reinforced, there seems to be a special framework that evolved across multiple decades. My hope is that interested readers will apply the framework plus their own variations and enhancements to make their Lean Startups a rip-roaring success. That would be the ultimate validation and the impact on what still is a big issue: the enormous innovation backlog.

For me the truly Rich Exit is the impact on our wonderful team, the reach of our products into the market, the validation of our ideas, the friendships forged with fond memories, and foremost the even greater momentum of all that as reflected in the testimonials that came fully twenty-one years after I left Kenan Systems, which had then become a wholly owned subsidiary of Lucent and Bell Labs.

By the way, I learned that some former staff many years ago formed a group, *Kenanites*, and they still meet regularly. I am now ready to join in and resume telling corny stories while I wear funny hats.

Successful journeys to all of us as we navigate the arid valleys successfully and then battle the unwelcoming occupants in the green valleys. May our jobs be fun, so it doesn't feel like work.

For me the truly Rich Exit is the impact on our wonderful team, the reach of our products into the market, the validation of our ideas, and the ability to give back to MIT, which gave so much to me.

Yes, the truly Rich Exit is in the gratitude that bursts out.

ABOUT THE AUTHOR

Dr. Kenan Sahin is an academic, scientist, inventor, technologist, serial entrepreneur, and philanthropist. Educated at Massachusetts Institute of Technology (BS, PhD), he went on to teach there as well as at the University of Massachusetts in Amherst (tenured), and at Harvard University. At MIT, Dr. Sahin received the Salgo-Noren Teaching Excellence Award. His focus has been business innovation and technology implementation, and he holds fundamental patents on communication networks and advanced materials.

Dr. Sahin founded Kenan Systems with $1,000 of his own funds and grew it into an international company with over a thousand employees, selling it as the sole shareholder to Lucent/Bell Labs for $1.5 billion. He then ran one of Lucent's commercial groups and became vice president of Technology at Bell Labs.

In 2002, Dr. Sahin founded TIAX with his own funds to acquire the lab-based Technology and Innovation unit of Arthur D. Little when it was restructured after 116 years of operations. In 2014, he spun out TIAX's Advanced Materials division as CAMX Power. He serves as president of TIAX and CAMX, with both companies continuing to play key roles in their domains.

Dr. Sahin's numerous awards include the World Economic Forum Technology Pioneer, the International Institute of Boston Golden Door Award, the Ellis Island Medal of Honor, the American

Academy of Achievement Golden Plate, and the Ernst & Young New England Entrepreneur of the Year. MIT's Dean of Humanities and Social Science and other professorships and fellowships have been endowed in his name.

Dr. Sahin's service on Boards extends to those of MIT (as a Life Member), Argonne National Laboratories, MIT Energy Initiative, NEMA, Boston Symphony, and Boston Museum of Fine Arts.

He now lives in Lincoln, works in Lexington, Massachusetts, and vacations in Kennebunkport, Maine, and Bodrum, Turkey.

ACKNOWLEDGMENTS AND DEDICATION

I am grateful to MIT for educating me as a total person, expanding my mind in science, technology, arts, and humanities, and making me an integral part of its ecosystem. I meant to stay only for a short time, but after sixty-two years I'm still embedded in the MIT ecosystem. My time with MIT has represented 40 percent of MIT's entire life span, commencing with an 1861 charter to be a "society of arts, a museum of arts and a school of industrial science," thus with a *portfolio of offers* that evolved through *noisy exploration*—two of the critical principles espoused in these pages and practiced in the Kenan Systems business experiment.

In the richly networked ecosystem of MIT, I was honored to work alongside many highly impactful people including its presidents, starting with Killian, then Stratton, Johnson, Wiesner, Gray, Vest, Hockfield, and Reif, along with the institution's chairmen of the Boards, including Johnson, D'Arbeloff, Mead, Reed, and Millard. Each was a mentor and colleague, with Johnson, Wiesner, and Vest serving on my company Boards.

Foremost, it was the MIT Sloan Fellows I taught (and who taught me) for fifteen years who are the inspirators, mentors, and enablers of the *Lean Startup, To Lean Company, To Rich Exit* that I chronicle here. Our original team of six at CMD were all MIT students—each joining for a summer and then remaining for the long haul and becoming pillars of CMD and later Kenan Systems, unsuspecting participants in the decades-long experiment I was running. Each was a true colleague as we navigated without a compass, map, or even a rudder, all too often in turbulent waters.

Subsequent hires from other world-class institutions were also exceptionally talented, dedicated, productive, and impactful. All of us became nodes in a richly interconnected matrix of talent that extended to CMD and again to Kenan Systems and now continue to drive innovation across industry.

Perhaps no better articulation of this expanding matrix can be found than the testimonials and remembrances offered by my colleagues and fellow *Kenanites* (a name they chose) in this book's Appendix.

This book is dedicated to all the Kenanites.

Back in 1886, another MIT student, Arthur D. Little, launched his namesake startup. It took him nearly twenty-five years to turn the corner and become what I believe was the first technology consulting and transfer company in the United States. In 1937, per Little's will, Arthur D. Little, Inc. (ADL) was gifted to MIT, where it was transformed into a greater technology powerhouse. In the early 1950s, ADL was spun out. Once again a private company, it expanded its size and impact. But the "original ADL" with its laboratories and focus on technology remained as the Technology and Innovation (T&I) unit. When ADL came to an end in 2002, I personally bought the assets of T&I quite by accident and then folded its existing staff of 250 into my startup TIAX (*Technology* and *Innovation Accelerated* with *X*, hence TIAX). Overnight, TIAX, the startup, morphed into a *Restart* of a heritage company that after 116 years was auctioned off in five parts, one being T&I. As it turned out, TIAX had been the only bidder for T&I. Subsequently, no outsiders wanted to invest. Thus, without any fiduciary responsibility, I was able to continue my decades-long validation, now in a *Restart setting.*

With the validation in an environment so intertwined with MIT, I asked Dr. Charles Vest, MIT's president at the time, to chair the TIAX Advisory Board. He honored me and TIAX for five years, until leaving MIT to become the president of the National Academy of Engineering. The *Restart* validation continues on and shall be chronicled in the next book.

I am deeply grateful to my family, particularly my sons, who became participants in this validation quest. A special gratitude to Kent, who gifted me the Zoom call on my eightieth birthday—which included my former colleagues and members of Bell Labs staff—twenty-two years after leaving Kenan Systems and two years after it merged into Lucent/Bell Labs.

That Zoom call transported me back in time and inspired me deeply. The 150 employees, and many more as well, were carrying the torch forward. It was then that I learned that the key product of Kenan Systems—Arbor/BP, renamed by Lucent as Kenan/BP—now services over a billion telco subscribers, or nearly 40 percent of the global market.

I am also grateful to Forbes Books. They put me on the path, with Lee Troxler designated as the ghostwriter. I chose to write the first draft myself—alas, in a dry, academic, lecturing manner. Lee rewrote it in a readable way and, as appropriate, added content. Then I rewrote it on to this final version—*expanding/contracting* or *diverging/converging* and *iterating/undulating.* I started out with an *initial offer set,* expanded through *noisy explorations* embodied in *undulations.* In a real sense, Lee is the contributing author; I have a deep appreciation for his work.

When I left Lucent in December 2000, almost all of my notes and records stayed behind, which means this book was written almost entirely from memory. Even as I express my deep gratitude to so many, I hope unintended omissions will be forgiven. That I remember so much, so vividly and fondly, is a testament to how well I was taught by the Sloan Fellows, Kenanites, the outstanding clients and partners, the mentors like Johnson, Wiesner, Vest, and so many others. Thank you all. I trust this book will effectively transmit the combined learnings to readers.

RESOURCES

1   "Chapter 2: Multijurisdictional mergers: Facilitating substantive convergence and minimizing conflict," Department of Justice, Updated June 25, 2015, https://www.justice.gov/atr/chapter-2

    and

    "The Top 100 Mergers and Acquisitions of 1999," NJBIZ, August 9, 2005, https://njbiz.com/the-top-100-mergers-and-acquisitions-of-1999/.

2   Stephen D. Oliner and Daniel E. Sichel, "The Resurgence of Growth in the Late 1990s: Is Information Technology the Story?" May 2000, https://www.federalreserve.gov/pubs/feds/2000/200020/200020pap.pdf.

3   Daniel Golden, "Billionaire Sahin Pledges Gift to MIT of $100 Million, School's Largest Ever," *Wall Street Journal*, November 9, 1999. https://www.wsj.com/articles/SB942114237709882801

4   The Salgo-Noren Foundation, "About the Salgo Trust for Education," https://salgotrust.org/about.

5   "Business Formation Statistics," Census.gov, n.d., https://www.census.gov/econ/bfs/index.html.

6   "Number of Business Establishments in the United States in March 2022, by Age," Statista, February 14, 2023, https://www.statista.com/statistics/873316/number-of-entrepreneurial-businesses-in-the-us-by-age/.

7   "Number of IPOs in the United States from 1999 to 2022," Statista, February 3, 2023, https://www.statista.com/statistics/270290/number-of-ipos-in-the-us-since-1999/.

8   Kerry Sun, "Half of All 2021 IPOs Underwater after Record Year for Listings," Market Index, December 31, 2021, https://www.marketindex.com.au/news/half-of-all-2021-ipos-underwater-after-record-year-for-listings.

9   Based on data compiled from the World Federation of Exchanges and the US Census Bureau.

10   "Number of Merger and Acquisition Transactions in the United States from 2020 to 2022, by Deal Value," Statista, May 22, 2023, https://www.statista.com/statistics/245977/number-of-munda-deals-in-the-united-states/

11   "Canadian Pacific and Kansas City Southern Combination Approved by U.S. Surface Transportation Board," Kansas City Southern, March 15, 2023, https://www.kcsouthern.com/media/news/news-releases/canadian-pacific-and-kansas-city-southern-combination-approved-by-u-s-surface-transportation-board.

12   Alex Lazarow, "Beyond Silicon Valley," *Harvard Business Review*, March–April 2020, https://hbr.org/2020/03/beyond-silicon-valley.

13   For more information on the talented Keith Sawyer, please visit: https://expertfile.com/experts/keith.sawyermaphd/keith-sawyer-ma-phd.

14   Rami Ayyub, "U.S. Student Test Results Show Toll of Pandemic Lockdowns on Learning," Reuters, October 25, 2022, https://www.reuters.com/world/us/us-student-test-results-document-pandemics-toll-learning-2022-10-24.

15   Joe Bower, "Kenan Systems," *Harvard Business Review*, December 15, 2010, https://www.hbs.edu/faculty/Pages/item.aspx?num=27871.

16 Satish Nambisan, "Why Service Businesses Are Not Product Businesses," *MIT Sloan Management Review*, Summer 2001, https://sloanreview.mit.edu/article/why-service-businesses-are-not-product-businesses/.

17 Tom Peters and Robert H. Waterman, *In Search of Excellence: Lessons from America's Best-Run Companies* (New York: HarperCollins, 2006), https://www.harpercollins.com/products/in-search-of-excellence-thomas-j-petersrobert-h-waterman.

18 Liz Ryan, "Ten Reasons Everybody Hates HR," *Forbes*, July 27, 2016, https://www.forbes.com/sites/lizryan/2016/07/27/ten-reasons-everybody-hates-hr.

19 Joe Bower, "Kenan Systems," *Harvard Business Review*, December 15, 2010, https://www.hbs.edu/faculty/Pages/item.aspx?num=27871.

20 See data at https://www.multpl.com/s-p-500-pe-ratio/table/by-year

21 Rita McGrath, "What Happens When CEOs Have Too Much Power," CNN Business Perspectives, November 29, 2018, https://www.cnn.com/2018/11/29/perspectives/facebook-mark-zuckerberg-nissan-carlos-ghosn-corporate-governance/index.html.

and

John Graham, "CEO Power and Board Dynamics," Harvard Law School Forum on Corporate Governance, Monday, April 3, 2017, https://corpgov.law.harvard.edu/2017/04/03/ceo-power-and-board-dynamics/

and

Parmy Olson, "Musk and Other Tech Billionaires Are Out of Control," Bloomberg, April 28, 2022, https://www.bloomberg.com/opinion/articles/2022-04-28/elon-musk-and-other-tech-billionaires-have-too-much-power.

APPENDIX B

MIT Sloan Management Review, 1991

APPLYING

BY AMIEL KORNEL

Can a business-school professor translate his academic experience into corporate success? Skeptics might argue that moving from towers of ivory to walls of brick and morter would befuddle even the most capable scholar.

Kenan Sahin SB '63, PhD '69 undertook just such a challenge when he left the Sloan School in 1983 to devote his time to Consultants for Management Decisions (CMD), the firm he had newly launched to provide clients with easy-to-use, custom developed decision support software tools. "As CMD evolved, it became clear to me that in many ways I would be able to practice what I had been teaching and preaching in academia," he says.

The contented staff and customers of the company—which changed its name in March to Kenan Systems Corp.—today attest to its founder's success. In fact, the company's approach to solving management problems with information system-based solutions is winning accolades. Additionally, its own innovative management policies have attracted top talent and, perhaps more importantly, motivated employees to stick with the company as it grows.

And grown it has. Sahin, who is both president and chairman, has parlayed his initial $1,000 investment into a business that garnered $7 million in revenues last year. The company has grown by 50 percent in the past twelve months and has been profitable since its inception, he says. Headquartered in Kendall Square in Cambridge just across the street from Sloan, Kenan Systems has additional offices in Denver, New York, and Washington, DC.

Managing growth while preserving the company's collegial atmosphere and non-hierarchical orientation has become one of the greatest challenges facing the firm. "It will be interesting to see whether the company can maintain its current culture and organization as it grows bigger," says Don Siegrist SM '84, who joined Kenan Systems in December 1990.

Founder, Chairman, President **Kenan Sahin**.

It is a key question since Kenan Systems' strong growth has proven to be a powerful lure for the talented people on which its continued success depends. "What's kept all of us here have been the changing management challenges as the company gets bigger," says Steve Dalton SM '84.

Long-standing MIT ties

Thirty of Kenan Systems' seventy-two staff members are MIT graduates, with two-thirds of them coming from Sloan. Dalton and five classmates from his Sloan graduating class joined the company nearly seven years ago. Despite the high job mobility common in consultancy, four of them continue to work there today.

The oldest Sloan graduate on staff is fifty-year-old Sahin himself, who earned his undergraduate degree at Sloan in 1963 after emigrating to the United States from Turkey in 1959, and the PhD degree in

1969. His doctoral work lead to worldwide patents in areas relating to neural networks and massively parallel computers.

His relationship with MIT since graduation has never stopped. Sahin held a faculty position at Sloan from 1967 to 1971 and periodically taught at the school as a visiting professor through 1983, including twelve classes of Sloan Fellows. From 1971 to 1983, he concurrently held a position as professor of Management at the University of Massachusetts at Amherst.

Developing software for management

"Management needs information, but what they often get is data," says Sahin. As a result, he explains, "Most management time is spent managing a process, not making a decision."

To move from business intentions to business decisions, you need a model of the organization, he explains. That model, he adds, then allows the firm to translate strategic plans into operational plans. The result is a powerful means for tailoring companies more closely to their business objectives.

"Systems like this can be used to re-configure the organization," says Sahin. He emphasizes that his consultants' recommendations and the software tools they develop do not require companies to change radically their way of doing business. "We had to master the art of overlaying and integrating, rather than bulldozing," he says.

He underscores Kenan Systems' "non-judgmental approach" to consulting. "We're not management consultants," he explains. "We're systems consultants." Although he and his staff must understand their clients' management processes in order to develop appropriate software systems, they avoid becoming advocates or opponents of specific management practices, he says.

In a recent departure from its exclusive focus on custom software development, Kenan Systems created a new product division, Templar Technolo-

BUSINESS THEORY

gies, that offers generic tools for enhancing the productivity of managers.

Innovative management practices

From the beginning, Sahin has employed innovative management techniques, thereby transforming Kenan Systems into a laboratory for the management concepts he explored previously as a professor.

Above all, the company has remained profoundly team-oriented and non-hierarchical. "This was the first place I found where there was truly—in deed as well as in word—a dedication to a democratic work environment," says Louis Gutierrez SM '90, who coordinates product development.

Eschewing the prerogative of absolute power normally reserved for a company's founder, Sahin created a Board of Directors that would evaluate his decisions and performance as well as serve to suggest strategic ideas. He preferred being "simply another employee" in his own company, he says.

Drawing on his academic contacts, he invited Howard Johnson, former dean of Sloan as well as chairman and president of MIT, and Jerome Wiesner, former president of MIT and science advisor to President Kennedy, to join him on the Board. Alan White, an associate dean at Sloan, later became the Board's fourth member.

Sahin's decision to make himself accountable to a higher authority reflects his belief that effective teamwork requires individuals who are prepared to follow as well as lead. "To cultivate a team organization, you need to cultivate the abilities to lead and be lead," he explains. This means staying away from perks and privileges. All Kenan Systems offices are shared unless business needs require a private office. Sahin reinforces this non-hierarchical approach to management through example. "When somebody goes out to pick up lunch for a meeting, he is as likely to volunteer as anyone," says Dalton.

Kenan Systems also has no pecking

W E'RE NOT MANAGEMENT CONSULTANTS, WE'RE SYSTEMS CONSULTANTS.

The Sloan contingent at Kenan Systems. Seated, *l* to *r*: David Watson SB '88, Mike Cebry SM '85, Steve Dalton SB '81, Joyce Pollack SB '82, Kenan Sahin '63 PhD '69, Don Siegrist SM '84. Standing, *l* to *r*: Steve Bernard SM '89, Velma Cone SM '89, Bob Karp SB '82 SM '86, Karen Troy SM '85, Louis Gutierrez SM '90, Fred Konopka SM '90, Mike Magras SB '85. Not pictured: Beth Reiland SM '84, John Ruggiero SM '82, Kurt Silverman SM '84, Mark Trusheim SM '84, Darren Walsh SM '84, Doug Ward SB '80.

order in the allocation of resources. Competence and business requirements take precedence over seniority. This approach encourages team building and easy reconfiguring of the organization for each project. "It assures that decisions we make are based on what is best for the business," explains Sahin.

The fact that a single billing rate is applied to all staff members also signals that no one individual is valued more than another, says Dalton.

Sahin, nonetheless, doesn't consider the organization of Kenan Systems flat. "Flat organizations either have no leaders or dictators," he says. Rather, at Kenan Systems, leadership develops from the needs of a particular project and the specific competences of the staff assembled to address it.

Staff allocation is handled monthly by two project managers who evaluate information about project funding levels and the project preferences of staff

9

234

members.

Employee performance reviews, until recently conducted by Sahin, are now being conducted by project managers. As teams group and regroup, however, the roles of evaluator and evaluee may be reversed. Sahin reviews the project managers.

Sahin has transferred more than management concepts from academia to his company. In general, he considers Kenan Systems a learning organization. "We have to be dedicated to talent and excellence," he says. "We have to be learning all the time." In hiring, he looks for generalists and quick learners who have a knack for system development but are not necessarily program developers.

Tackling the problems of large organizations worldwide

Many of Kenan Systems' clients are large organizations in such industries as telecommunications, financial services, and government. Contracts have ranged in value from $50,000 to $1 million. Targeting these markets puts Kenan Systems into direct competition with many of the largest consultancies, including McKinsey & Co., Booz Allen & Hamilton, Arthur D. Little, and the big accounting firms.

Kenan Systems developed its Model for Evaluating Technological Alternatives (META) to allow the U.S. Postal Service to evaluate different technologies and implementation scenarios for its $13 billion automation plan currently underway and scheduled for completion in the mid-1990's. The automation program will "void" the need to hire an additional 135,000 workers in coming years as mail volume continues to rise, says Fred Dilisio, director of Operations Research at the Postal Service.

Last Spring, Kenan Systems finished an automation model that will generate operations planning for each of the Postal Service's seventy-three divisions nationwide. It has also developed prototypes of a supervisor's workstation, an expert system that helps manage sorting at each mail-processing facility. "It allows control of mail flow across the floor," says Dilisio.

Finally, Kenan Systems designed a workflow planning model that helps lay out each facility by evaluating the impact on labor of the physical movement of mail from one area to another.

In recognition of the quality of its work, Kenan Systems last year was one of eleven companies to receive a citation as a "Quality Supplier" to the U.S. Post Office. The Post Office is one of the country's largest distribution service providers and uses more than 70,000 suppliers.

On the financial services front, Kenan Systems has received contracts from Citibank since 1983 for various projects including a decision-support software system for analysing credit applications from Savings and Loans.

The CitiExpert software Kenan Systems developed for Citibank uses a rule-based expert system and concepts from linguistic semantics to route and process unstructured telex messages received by banks for funds transfers. This software is at the core of an intelligent banking system now marketed by the company which also can handle other types of financial transactions. It has been licensed to telecommunications service providers TRT and AT&T.

Elsewhere in the telecommunications sector, Kenan Systems has also developed an artificial intelligence-based, automated bill-correction system for regional Bell operating company U.S. West.

The company's reach extends beyond U.S. shores. Teijiun Ltd, a large Japanese company selling polyester film used for recording media, asked Sahin's firm to produce a system for product profitability simulation and planning. Finished in 1989, it allows the company to review production on a monthly basis. In Europe, Kenan Systems has been developing a relationship with British Telecom, the principal telecommunications services provider in the U.K., and has already delivered two software systems for strategic planning.

Kenan Systems staff members speak enthusiastically of the diverse and intellectually stimulating projects they encounter in their jobs. More than anything, perhaps, they feel this is what sets the company apart from other consultancies. Maintaining such a challenging environment has been largely possible, they note, because Sahin remains the privately-held firm's majority shareholder. Relying exclusively on internally-generated financing has allowed him to focus on long-term strategy rather than short-term returns on investment.

"Kenan doesn't drive the business as a revenue generator," says Gutierrez, "but on fundamental values such as: Are we delivering quality service and meeting customer expectations? Are we enjoying working here? The rest takes care of itself, or at least it has up to this point."

As the company grows, the need to maintain focus on those basic questions will no doubt further test Sahin's knack for transferring academic ideas about management to the pragmatic world of business. ∎

WE HAVE TO BE LEARNING ALL THE TIME.

Advanced facer/cancellers are part of the new generation of automated sorting equipment being deployed by the U.S. Postal Service. Kenan Systems' modelling work has played an integral part in determining equipment acquisitions to meet Postal automation goals.

Amiel Kornel, "Applying Business Theory," *MIT Sloan Management Review*, 1991.

Conference On Innovative Applications Of Artificial Intelligence,
1989

The Intelligent Banking System

Dr. Kenan Sahin and Keith Sawyer

Consultants for Management Decisions, Inc.
One Broadway
Cambridge, MA 02142

Abstract

This paper describes the Intelligent Banking System (IBS), a family of applications developed for Citibank, New York, by Consultants for Management Decisions (CMD) to increase the productivity and effectiveness of English text message processing. These messages were previously processed manually. Data entry operators would read and analyze the message and then type information at a standard ASCII terminal interface. IBS applies a combination of natural language processing and rule-based expert system techniques to analyze the message and to generate a formatted equivalent. IBS also provides a sophisticated intelligent user interface which aids users by applying the system's domain knowledge to the interactive session.

Introduction

International Banking relies heavily on the electronic transfer of messages for basic transactions. Until the mid-seventies, messages were transmitted over the telex carrier networks, as natural language text. In the mid- to late-seventies, the major international banks developed several industry-wide structured formats to represent the most common banking messages, such as funds transfers. This then allowed the banks to develop computer software which could automatically process the structured transaction, precluding the need for manual intervention. (This parallels the more recent moves to EDI in other industries.)

Despite the widespread success of this strategy in reducing processing costs and increasing bank productivity, a significant minority of the international message traffic remained natural language text. This traffic still required costly and error-prone manual processing. Proficient operators needed a significant understanding of international banking transactions, creating high training costs and limiting staffing flexibility.

Because of the need to process English text input, and the need to incorporate a significant amount of domain expertise, traditional programming techniques were inadequate. Artificial Intelligence technology was identified as the appropriate solution. AI offers two groups of techniques which are used by IBS: *Natural Language Processing* techniques, and *Rule-based Expert System* techniques.

The goal of the Intelligent Banking System (IBS) is to use a combination of these techniques to allow the computer to scan and "understand" a natural language text message. Automating the task in this manner would reduce banking costs, increase operator productivity, and reduce the chance of manual error. The task seemed appropriate for this technology, since the application satisfied many of the accepted criteria (Davis, 1982, and Prerau, 1985):

- The domain is characterized by the use of expert knowledge, judgement and experience

- Conventional programming solutions are inadequate

- There are recognized experts that solve the problem today

- The completed system is expected to have a significant payoff for the corporation

- The task requires the use of heuristics, or "rules of thumb"

- The task is neither too easy nor too difficult

- The system can be phased into use gracefully

Kenan Sahin, "The Intelligent Banking System," in *Conference on Innovative Applications of Artificial Intelligence* (Menlo Park, CA: American Association for Artificial Intelligence, 1989).

Financial Times, January 12, 1999

FINANCIAL TIMES

COMPANIES & MARKETS

© THE FINANCIAL TIMES LIMITED 1999   TUESDAY JANUARY 12 1999   Week 2

ACQUISITION OF TELECOMS SOFTWARE MAKER COMES HARD ON HEELS OF REPORTS OF IMMINENT MERGER WITH ASCEND

Lucent to buy Kenan for $1.5bn

By Roger Taylor in San Francisco, William Lewis in New York and Alan Cane in London

Lucent Technologies, the world's largest telecommunications equipment manufacturer, yesterday announced the $1.48bn acquisition of Kenan Systems, a leading maker of telephone billing and customer care software.

The announcement came as Lucent investors were digesting the disclosure in the Financial Times that Lucent is close to announcing a merger with Ascend Communications, a US data networking group.

Yesterday both Lucent and Ascend declined to comment

but people close to the talks said the deal remained on track to be announced within days.

On Wall Street yesterday Ascend's share price closed up $5¼ at $76⅝, giving it a market capitalisation of more than $16bn, while Lucent shares fell $2⅜ to $113⅜.

Shares in Alcatel, the French telecoms manufacturer which announced an alliance with Ascend six months ago, fell €8.70, or more than 5 per cent, to €115 on the news of the link-up. Analysts said an acquisition would damage Alcatel's competitive position as well as casting doubts over the future of the alliance.

The news also moved the stock prices of European competitors, with Siemens of Germany up €0.30 at €61.10, Ericsson of Sweden down SKr5 at SKr206.50 and Nokia of Finland up €0.59 at €118.99.

Discussing the Kenan acquisition yesterday, Dan Stanzione, chief operating officer at Lucent, said it fitted well with the company's strategy of targeting the fastest-growing parts of the telecoms market.

He said the communications software market was growing at 25 per cent a year and would be worth about $26bn in 2000. Kenan Systems is the leading provider of third party billing and customer care soft-

ware, a market growing at 30 per cent a year. He added billing and services software was the area in which telephone companies had the greatest need for better products.

With the growth of competition in the telecoms sector, operators were increasingly seeking to differentiate themselves by the quality of their billing – for instance, the ability to itemise a bill and analyse a customer's spend in different ways. Kenan's software can, for example, recognise trends and give early warning that a customer may be preparing to leave the network.

Mr Stanzione would not comment on the talks with

Ascend but confirmed that Lucent was interested in acquiring data networking businesses. Both deals would help Lucent provide equipment to telephone companies anxious to offer complete services to corporate customers, handling both traditional telephone calls as well as computer data traffic.

The sudden increase in activity by Lucent reflects rapid consolidation in the market for telecommunications equipment and the relaxation of accounting restrictions.

Kenan Sahin, president and sole owner of Kenan Systems, will join Lucent and help with product development.

Roger Taylor, William Lewis, and Alan Cane, "Lucent to Buy Kenan for $1.5bn," *Financial Times*, January 12, 1999.

Boston Herald, January 12, 1999

Business

TUESDAY, JANUARY 12, 1999 . BOSTON HERALD   23

The bill for Kenan: $1.5B

By TODD WALLACK

Massachusetts gained another billionaire yesterday.

Entrepreneur Kenan Sahin agreed to sell his fast-growing Cambridge software company to Lucent Technologies Inc. for about $1.5 billion in stock.

Kenan Systems Corp., with 750 workers, provides billing and order software for telephone companies and Internet service providers. The 15-year-old company had about $175 million in sales last year, up from $100 million the year before.

Sahin, a former Harvard and MIT professor who owns 100 percent of Kenan, said he plans to use the bulk of his new wealth to set up a foundation to distribute educational software.

Employees won't profit directly from the sale, but many will receive financial incentives to stay on. "No one really joined our company to get rich," Sahin said.

Lucent, based in Murray Hill, N.J. said Kenan will give it a foothold in the fast-growing market for communications billing software. "That's a space where we haven't played before," said Dan Stanzione, Lucent's chief operating officer.

In addition, Kenan could help boost Lucent's European sales. Kenan claims 40 percent of its sales from overseas. Lucent shares slipped $2.31 to $112.94 on the news. Paul Hughes, an analyst with the Yankee Group in Boston, said he thinks the sale could push other telecommunications firms to invest in billing software or make similar deals.

"It's not a very sexy marketplace," Hughes said, "but billing is extremely important to (telecommunications) service providers. It is the primary way they communicate with customers."

Despite Kenan's growth, the company has kept a low profile and spurned possible buyers in the past.

"We jealously guarded our priva-

Turn to Page 28

Lucent hooks up with Kenan for $1.5B

From Page 23

cy," Sahin said.

But Sahin said Kenan now needs to team up with a larger partner to maintain its growth.

Lucent said it first approached the company about a sale a few months ago as part of partnership talks. The deal is expected to close by March 31.

Executives said the deal will add a few pennies a share to earnings this year.

Most billing software firms enjoy pre-tax profit margins of 20 percent to 30 percent of revenue.

Sahin will continue to run the firm, which will remain in Cambridge as a subsidiary of Lucent. Executives also said they will transfer 100 Lucent software developers to Kenan.

Meanwhile, rumors continued to swirl that Lucent was in talks to buy Ascend Communications Inc. for roughly $16 billion.

Analysts have speculated Lucent would target Ascend, a California company with significant Massachusetts operations.

But the speculation went into overdrive over the week- end on published reports that they were in talks and could announce a deal this week.

Ascend has about 1,130 local workers.

Sale pending

Lucent Technologies Inc., the world's largest phone-equipment maker, is buying closely held Kenan Systems Corp., which makes billing-systems software, for about $1.48 billion.

Lucent Technologies

- **Headquarters:** Murray Hill, N.J.
- **Employees:** 141,600
- **Revenue:** $3.01 billion
- **Chairman:** Richard A. McGinn
- **Formed:** 1996 (AT&T spinoff)

K·E·N·A·N

- **Headquarters:** Cambridge
- **Employees:** 750
- **Revenue:** $75 million
- **Founder, CEO:** Kenan Sahin
- **Founded:** 1982

Source: Herald research

STAFF GRAPHIC BY MICHAEL BERTRAND

Todd Wallack, "The Bill for Kenan: $1.5b," *The Boston Herald*, January 12, 1999.

The New York Times, January 12, 1999

THE NEW YORK TIMES, TUESDAY, JANUARY 12, 1999   YNE   C9

Lucent to Buy Kenan for $1.45 Billion, but Is Quiet on Possible Acquisition of Ascend

By BARNABY J. FEDER
and LAURA M. HOLSON

Lucent Technologies said yesterday that it would buy the Kenan Systems Corporation, a leader in billing software, but declined to talk about the far bigger deal on Wall Street's mind, a possible acquisition of Ascend Communications Inc., a leading data communications equipment maker.

Lucent, the former telephone equipment manufacturing arm of AT&T, said it would acquire all of Kenan from its founder and president, Kenan Sahin, for 12.88 million shares valued at $1.45 billion, based on yesterday's closing prices. Shares of Lucent fell $2.50, to $112.75.

The 57-year-old Mr. Sahin will become a vice president at Lucent's Bell Labs research center and continue to run the billing software business from Kenan's headquarters in Cambridge, Mass. He said that the bulk of his suddenly public fortune would go to a new foundation dedicated to converting college-level classroom courses into interactive software that would be distributed around the world.

Kenan develops software that allows phone companies like MCI Worldcom and AT&T Worldnet to provide a single bill covering a variety of services, including regular and wireless phone, data transmission, Internet and broadband cable.

The software also manages new service orders and helps clients design and simulate new pricing and service plans. Phone companies are eager to have flexible billing systems to bundle services and quickly adjust marketing plans because customers are less likely to jump to rivals if they buy several services.

Kenan's sales have been doubling annually in recent years, reaching $175 million last year, Mr. Sahin said. Lucent said that the billing software niche was growing 30 percent a year, faster than the broader $20 billion communications software market.

"We decided to jump to the head of the pack by acquiring the hottest player in the business," said Daniel C. Stanzione, executive vice president and chief operating officer of Lucent, based in Murray Hill, N.J.

Analysts liked the deal. Kenan is expected to add at least 3 cents a share to Lucent's earnings in the current year ending Sept. 30, which should hit $2.11 a share, according to the First Call Corporation's consensus estimate from 27 analysts. Lucent earned $548 million, or 41 cents a diluted share before special charges, on revenue of $8 billion in the quarter ended Sept. 30.

Lucent's strong position in the old regional Bell companies is likely to generate new opportunities for Kenan. Meanwhile, Kenan's overseas presence — now 40 percent of its revenue — should open doors for Lucent equipment and services as it battles with rivals like Alcatel of France and Siemens of Germany for market share.

"It was a great acquisition for Lucent," said Greg Geiling, who follows Lucent for J. P. Morgan.

Still, it was not the primary deal on investors' minds. The drop in Lucent shares was driven by nervousness about a possible deal with Ascend. Based on current valuations, such a deal would be 10 times pricier than the Kenan acquisition.

Speculation has been rampant for more than a year that Lucent might someday buy Ascend as it prepares to take on Cisco Systems, the giant of data networking. As data networks like the Internet and phone networks converge so that the same services can be offered over both, newcomers like Cisco and Ascend are increasingly competing directly with traditional telecommunications equipment makers like Lucent and Northern Telecom.

Lucent is continuing its talks with Ascend Communications, which were first reported in The Financial Times, although it is not known if or when an announced deal is likely, people close to the talks said.

The companies have had talks over the last several months, but Ascend had always asserted it could remain independent. In a recent October conference call with analysts, Mory Ejabat, the president and chief executive officer of Ascend, evaded the topic of a buyout and said his company was then not having talks with Lucent executives.

"It was kind of like saying I have not had sexual relations with that woman Monica Lewinsky," said Paul Sagawa, a senior research analyst at Sanford C. Bernstein, who took part in the conference call. "It was so clearly a Clintonesque response."

An Ascend acquisition would also be a departure from what Ken Fehrnstrom, vice president for strategic business development for Ascend, said in an interview late last month. He reiterated Ascend's desire to remain independent and compared the company to a "small dog that doesn't know it's a small dog; it will go after the big dogs." He also joked, "Maybe some day we could acquire Nortel," referring to Lucent's $36 billion Canadian rival Northern Telecom.

What's Sunday without The Times?

Barnaby Feder and Laura Holson, "Lucent to Buy Kenan for $1.45 Billion, but Is Quiet on Possible Acquisition of Ascend," *The New York Times*, January 12, 1999.

Wall Street Journal, November 9, 1999

Billionaire Sahin Offers MIT Gift Of $100 Million

By DANIEL GOLDEN

Staff Reporter of THE WALL STREET JOURNAL

Software billionaire Kenan Sahin pledged $100 million to the Massachusetts Institute of Technology, the largest gift in the university's history.

Mr. Sahin's is the latest in a string of big donations by entrepeneurs in information technology and is thought to be only the beginning of a wave of stock-market-fueled philanthropy bigger than any since the days of the Carnegies, Vanderbilts and Rockefellers.

Among recent high-tech education benefactors, the 58-year-old Mr. Sahin joins entrepreneur James H. Clark, who gave $150 million to Stanford University last month; Microsoft Corp. Chairman Bill Gates, whose foundation recently promised $1 billion in college scholarships to minority students; and E*Trade Group Inc. founder Bill Porter, who gave $25 million to MIT's business school last month. Mr. Sahin sold his closely held company, Kenan Systems Corp., to Lucent Technologies Inc. in January for $1.48 billion.

Paul Schervish, a sociologist at Boston College, said that unlike the wealthy of the past, new philanthropists are choosing to concentrate their resources on one or a few beneficiaries—much as they concentrate their business energies on a single enterprise. The vast gifts, he said, are redefining philanthropy. "These fortunes are so huge that they become minigovernments in themselves," he said. "It's not philanthropy in the mode of supporting alongside other contributions. It's world building."

Mr. Sahin, whose pledge helped kick off a five-year, $1.5 billion MIT fund-raising campaign, said 70% of his gift is unrestricted, while 30% will be used to match other gifts in areas that he and a committee of four MIT leaders deem crucial.

A native of Turkey, Mr. Sahin received his bachelor's degree and doctorate from MIT and also taught there before founding Kenan Systems in 1982.

Mr. Sahin's gift came at a gala dinner Saturday to celebrate the launch of MIT's campaign. Mr. Sahin had planned to be in China to address its national academy of sciences, but the trip was postponed.

"I went over to [MIT President] Chuck Vest, and said, 'If you let me on the stage for a few moments, I want to make an announcement," Mr. Sahin said. "He asked what it was about, and I told him it was a surprise."

MIT's campaign is meant to raise money for student scholarships, building and a range of scientific study, including neurosciences, education and health technology and biotechnology programs.

Mr. Sahin also said he plans to start a foundation that will translate academic textbooks into interactive software for global use.

Daniel Golden, "Billionaire Sahin Offers MIT Gift Of $100 Million," *Wall Street Journal*, November 9, 1999.

Kenan demonstrating the value of the umbrella hat at a Kenan Systems get together.

Kenan with Howard Johnson, chairman of the Board of Kenan Systems and president
and chairman of MIT.

Kenan with Dr. Charles Vest, at the time president of MIT and chairman of the TIAX Advisory Board.

Kenan with Howard Johnson, former president of MIT, at the time chairman of the MIT Board and chairman of Kenan Systems board (center), and Dr. Jerome Wiesner, former president of MIT, at the time member of the Kenan Systems board (right).

SATELLITE BROADCAST SERIES

Presents

KENAN SAHIN
WILL KEYNOTE
OCTOBER
BROADCAST

**Kenan Systems:
Becoming a $Billion
Software Company
and Managing
Its Future**

**With
Moderator**

HOWARD
JOHNSON

"How to grow a startup"

"How to build to the next growth step"

*"How to create a retention approach
to knowledge and talent"*

*"How to shape life after the liquidity
event"*

**MIT'S KRESGE AUDITORIUM
THURSDAY, OCTOBER 5, 2000**

6:00 pm Registration - 7:00 pm Broadcast - 8:00 pm Q & A - 9:00 pm Reception

Invited to keynote the October 2000 MIT Enterprise Forum, with Howard Johnson moderating, Dr. Sahin spoke about growing a startup, taking a company to the next level, retaining talent, and shaping a life after a liquidity event. Having just merged Kenan Systems with Lucent, Dr. Sahin told a packed auditorium of young entrepreneurs that when a substantial exit does happen and money is no longer a concern, one becomes a custodian of that money and is now tasked with ensuring its highest and best use.

Bell Labs News, May 2000

An Interview with Kenan Sahin

Lucent: A Software Powerhouse 'Under the Hood'

BY STEPHEN J. HUDIK

It was just over a year ago that the Lucent acquisition of Kenan Systems of Cambridge, Mass. was completed. Kenan Systems' founder and owner, Kenan Sahin, received approximately $1.5 billion in Lucent common stock for his company. The purchase enabled Sahin to join forces with a large company like Lucent so that his small company could continue to grow and flourish. Today, Sahin maintains a dual role: as president of Kenan Systems, which operates as a Lucent subsidiary, and as vice president of Software Technology at Bell Labs. Steve Hudik of the BLN sat down with Sahin recently to discuss what's happened over the past year.

What was your perception of Lucent and Bell Labs before coming here?

From my academic days, I had some interaction with Bell Labs. MIT has a long history of interaction with Bell Labs. I knew its history and contributions. My own perception was that Bell Labs was an enormously talented and innovative organization, but had struggled after divestiture and the spin-off from AT&T. I thought of Lucent as a hardware company only.

You were approached by several companies wanting to purchase Kenan Systems and had turned down a previous offer from Lucent. What prompted you to change your mind?

Kenan Systems was fiercely independent and very successful by any metric. I had many discrete inquiries but I immediately discouraged them. I originally got together with Lucent to explore some joint partnering opportunities. At that time, Lucent expressed an interest in acquiring my company but I declined. I said no because I still perceived Lucent as a hardware-only company that didn't understand software.

After a series of very successful meetings in Europe, I flew back to London in June. I like to walk a lot and took a long walk when I started to think about my company's future.

I came to two decisions. The first was that Kenan Systems couldn't continue to grow as fast as we had been growing alone — about 60–70 percent annually — and still make our customers successful going it alone. The second was that Lucent was the only possible company I met with regarding a possible merger that might be a match. But without conducting some due diligence after our first discussions, I declined.

As part of the joint work we were doing with Lucent, a team of Kenan employees went down to Bell Labs. I asked them for their opinions about the chemistry of a potential match. They told me they felt an instant bonding. A team from Bell Labs had come up to Cambridge and reported the same thing.

As part of these ongoing discussions, I had learned a lot more about Lucent. I realized Lucent, under the hood, was a powerful software company whose potential wasn't fully realized. I thought we could accomplish a lot together.

I called Carl Hsu who was then heading the Software Group and told him I'd like to talk about

continued on page 4

SAHIN

continued from page 1

a merger. He told me the call was just in time as Lucent was very close to making other arrangements. So we restarted the whole process.

How has the transition gone for you and Kenan Systems employees?

The environment at Kenan Systems was very open. I didn't just make all the decisions but typically socialized the options with many people. But the decision to merge was a decision that only I could make.

The week after the announcement was made was a rough one. A lot of people were shocked and stunned.

To their credit, people gave it a chance. We did not experience a mass exodus or riots. In my initial comments, I told the people I didn't make the decision for money but rather so our work could make more of a difference. We'd gain an expanded staff and better development opportunities.

Some doubted that a company of 750 people could survive as a part of a much larger entity. But I had confidence we could make a change in the marketplace and within Lucent. And it has happened.

One difficulty involved timing. I asked for a "soft landing" after the merger, feeling we should go slowly when bringing a small company culture into a large company culture. Instead the period was rushed and created some issues. Overall, I'd say it's gone well.

Sometimes in large organizations, positions are misunderstood. My passion for software may have come across as a passion for independence. That's not

the case. Otherwise I wouldn't be here.

I have a great deal of confidence in Bell Labs and Lucent. I believe we have an opportunity to make fundamental and long-lasting changes in the software field.

Can you identify a few things that have become possible because of Bell Labs that Kenan Systems could not accomplish on its own?

Before the merger, we were focused tightly on the telecomm industry. We viewed ourselves as a software factory. Our research resources were very limited.

After the merger, some products such as Billdats came into the Kenan portfolio. In a few months, we picked up technology from Bell Labs that enabled our products to become much more real-time, which is especially relevant to the Internet market. We then picked up development platforms enabling us to move toward next generation products.

Because of the merger, Lucent now has software that focuses on three key areas: operations support, business support and analysis. No one comes close to that. Inside a year, the combination of Kenan Systems and Lucent's software group has a portfolio that is very much in demand.

Many operators emphasize the network and then realize they lack the software components to extract its value. They lack good order entry systems and can't respond to demand. It's a tragedy for them because they've created high-demand services but can't take orders or provision. That really frustrates customers. It's like going to a store seeing what you want but being told you can't buy it.

We've also set up a development and delivery center with Bell Labs, incorporating technology from the labs into our product set. It's been well received by customers and we expect to expand it. It's been helpful both to the researchers and the product development teams too.

What are some key challenges for Lucent and the software industry in particular?

There are several. Improving network interoperability is important. Networks used to be very distinct — one for wireless, one for voice and separate ones for cable and video. Now cable is broadband and can carry voice too. Wireless systems also have multiple purposes besides voice. Software needs to operate across those networks.

Another challenge is to implement a sales model where software is viewed as a high margin product. That requires a change in thinking. The traditional model was to sell the network and give away the software. If you do that today, you lose profitability.

We need to anticipate where the markets will be rather than react to them. If we're reacting, we'll lose. When we do come to market, we need to execute quickly. And we need to come to market in a sustainable way with a sales model that will reinforce the products. If the sales model calls for extensive customization and services, then you lose the margins. The product, its deployment and the sales model must all be in sync or we'll frustrate customers who have other choices.

What's your view on the communications network of the future?

Some people think the future will be dehumanizing. I

think otherwise. It will be more humanizing as we more rapidly move away from centralization and more toward decentralization. This will make things more personal.

On the access side, I see devices becoming more incorporated into our natural ways, such as glasses, tiny cameras and cell phones in jackets or shirts. Chips will connect you to a host of personal learning devises.

I see three "C's:" Communications, Computing and Content.

In the late 20th century, we achieved a combination of communication and computing. But the real change is the third "C" — when content is more directly incorporated into these devices on a personal level.

How would you describe your current role and responsibilities?

I practiced academia for a decade and then business for a decade. My real job has just begun. I'm here to bring value-add to the corporation and to convert our wonderful ideas to products.

I have two roles. As part of Bell Labs, I'm here to brainstorm with my colleagues and to look to the future. Simultaneously, I've got to be in the present, crashing to earth and helping to make sales.

I enjoy both roles. Some people don't. I enjoy the forward-thinking research and the business side. I actively participate in both. I enjoy interacting with people and have been involved in recruiting people — both in spotting talent and helping talent take shape. And Lucent is a very fertile place to attract people to.

I've taken a leading role in recruiting. I look for aptitude first, then attitude, a willingness to learn and if there's experience that's a bonus. That intellectual curiosity must always be there.

Ads in newspapers stress experience but I think a certain skill set — which includes wanting to learn and the ability to work in teams to transfer knowledge — is more important.

If you only have solitary workers and foster the concept of gurus, that means there's not enough sharing of information and the customers suffer. In product development you need to have that sharing.

You've often spoken about the value of education in shaping society and individual lives. Can you elaborate on that?

Education is a great simplifier and also a great homogenizer. It's a great unifier — the type of electrical engineering you practice in Massachusetts is not that much different than what is practiced in California. The same can be said about law or medicine. Education also creates powerful social and professional networks.

I believe strongly in promoting education. I try to do my share. After I left academia, I remained very active in recruiting. My role as an educator never ended. I'm pleased that my contribution to MIT has triggered other gifts to colleges.

In due time, I hope to form an institute that will take a leading role in converting curricular knowledge to software. It would involve a switch from the textbook as the chief medium of conveying knowledge to software. The advantages are the amount of information which can be stored and the ability to instantly update that information. ∎

Ed. Note: Kenan Sahin recently gave $100 million to MIT.

Stephen Hudik, "Lucent: A Software Powerhouse 'Under the Hood,'" *Bell Lab News*, 2000.